6.50

HOUSE OF

AF765633

LOCATION R

AUTHOR SIMPSON

Acc DATE

Pornography & Politics

DATE OF CATALOGUING

26 JAN 84

HOUSE OF COMMONS LIBRARY

TO BE
DISPOSED
BY
AUTHORITY

House of Commons Library

54056001025763

A.W.B. SIMPSON

Pornography & Politics:

A Look Back to the Williams Committee

LOCATION
Censorship
AUTHOR
SIMPSON
DATE of CATALOGUING
26 JAN 84
HOUSE OF COMMONS LIBRARY

WATERLOW PUBLISHERS LIMITED

First Edition 1983
© AWB Simpson 1983
Waterlow Publishers Ltd
Maxwell House
74 Worship St
London EC2A 2EN
A member of the British Printing &
Communication Corporation PLC

All rights reserved. No part of this
publication may be reproduced, stored in a retrieval
system or transmitted in any form or by any means
electronic mechanical photocopying recording or
otherwise without the prior permission of
Waterlow Publishers Limited.

ISBN 0 08-039156 7

Simpson, Brian
Pornography and politics
1. Pornography – Social aspects
I. Title
363.4'7 HQ471

ISBN 0 08-039156 7

HOUSE OF COMMONS
LIBRARY
CATALOGUED

Designed by The Graphic Partnership
Printed in Great Britain by
A. Wheaton & Co Ltd
Hennock Road Exeter EX2 8RP

Preface

I was a member of the Home Office Departmental Committee on Obscenity and Film Censorship, whose report was published in 1979 (Cmnd. 7772); the committee is usually called the Williams Committee, after its Chairman Professor Bernard Williams, now Provost of King's College Cambridge. In this book I have attempted to set out an account of what the committee did and how it set about its task, and what has happened in this branch of the law since. It is in some ways a depressing story, but members of government committees must assume a certain detachment in these matters, and this I have tried to do. It may yet happen that this branch of the law will be reformed by some future government, and in the meantime at least the report of the committee furnishes a very comprehensive review of the subject even for those not wholly convinced by all its arguments. Ranters will of course continue to rant, and for them this book may provide useful target material.

A.W.B. Simpson
August 1983

Foreword

by Rt. Hon. S C Silkin QC

The laws relating to the written, spoken and visual representation of the pornographic, indecent and obscene are anomalous, devoid of clear principle or objective and often unenforceable. They have been described, both from the judicial Bench and from the Parliamentary benches, as a mess, a morass, a quagmire. It is often a matter of chance whether the pornographer receives large profits, a destruction order or a prison sentence. In Parliament I have heard this uncertainty praised as a virtue of the system – or lack of system. Under that novel constitutional doctrine lack of certainty as to how the law will be applied leads to greater caution. Experience hardly bears this out. What it certainly leads to is a willingness to take risks for the high profits available to the entrepreneur in pornographic material. Pornography today is big business.

The law enforcement officer, from the policeman making a test purchase in a suburban shop to the Attorney-General deciding whether or not to sanction a prosecution, is in an unenviable position. He is well aware of society's pressures – from one direction to clamp down on licence, from the other to sustain freedom of expression. His personal predilections must be put aside. Whether he as an individual finds the material before him offensive, innocuous or perhaps even pleasurable, he must disregard his own sensations. His duty is to make the best judgement he can on whether the law has been broken, and if it has, whether the public interest requires the apparatus of the law to be brought to bear. In reaching a judgement on this second question he must bear in mind the well-known unpredictability of juries trying this type of case and the potential effect upon the public's respect for law of an acquittal or a series of acquittals. He must take account even of the possible occurrence of such an absurdity as that the same film, book or magazine may be the subject of a conviction by one jury and an acquittal by another – perhaps even contemporaneously. That absurdity is not mere fantasy; it has happened. What he must not do is to disregard the law because he personally may regard it as wrong-headed, anomalous or even perverse.

Citizens who are not learned in the law, and even some who are, find it difficult to understand the difference between the terms in frequent use – pornographic, indecent, obscene and others. Pornography, the word in most common everyday use, implies no offence known to the law. Indecent and obscene imply offences of widely different meaning; and each word itself may bear a different meaning in different contexts. These differences are of historical origin and are incapable of rational explanation. In this country the obscene cannot lawfully be published, but the indecent, however, cannot lawfully be imported. Was Parliament intending to encourage the market for home-produced indecencies which fell short of obscenity? Many people might regard the words as synonymous. The law does not. For "obscene" Parliament has adopted the test of whether the material in question has a tendency to deprave and corrupt, a test borrowed from the common law. No similar test applies to "indecent". In respect of obscene material Parliament has provided the "public good" defence. No such defence avails the indecent. Obscene articles may be destroyed by magistrate's order; and in practice no "public good" defence avails the owner or the publisher. To correct that anomaly Ministerial undertaking to Parliament has added other anomalies. For a limited safeguard against destruction is afforded to some who volunteer to face criminal trial by jury to enable the "public good" defence to be raised.

The complex problems raised by the resulting mix of law and Ministerial undertaking are not lessened by the "deprave and corrupt" test. It is a standard joke among those professionally involved in law enforcement in the field of pornography that few people could be less likely to be depraved and corrupted by what they see than the hardened police officers or DPP lawyers who customarily inspect the more highly publicized or controversial works. But the reality is, as the Williams Committee concluded on the mass of evidence before it, that an objective person cannot safely conclude that pornographic material has a tendency to deprave and corrupt anybody. Yet the public widely assumes the contrary and the courts are bound by law to assume it. As Attorney-General I found this branch of the law sufficiently troublesome to cause me to seek what enlightenment I could from those prepared to express an informed opinion. But apparently informed opinions varied and some were obviously based upon received concepts rather than objective analysis. As profits from pornography grew, so problems multiplied. It became clear, for instance, that the public was not so much concerned to avoid the risk of being depraved and corrupted as to avoid the environmental damage, caused by excessive emphasis on sex, to such areas as Soho, once a pleasant area to stroll through, but latterly altered beyond recognition by strip joints, alluring nude advertisements and the – possibly exaggerated – portrayal outside of salacious entertainment within. The damage was one of taste rather than depravity; to walk through such areas had become distasteful to the sensitive citizens who were in no danger of becoming depraved by the distasteful things which visually assaulted them. The law knew of no way of restoring such areas to their previous pleasant character. All that it could do, and did, was to search for and pursue the material whose tendency might be thought by the courts to deprave and corrupt; material more likely to be out of sight within such establishments than outside advertising the delights within. So the chimera of the depraving and corrupting was rigorously pursued, even to the extent of the actual corruption of some police officers, whilst the visual assault on the taste and sensibilities of the passer-by was ignored.

This was the situation which led to the establishment of the Williams Committee, of which Professor Simpson was a distinguished legal member. The Attorney-General, constitutionally responsible for prosecution policy and specifically for some, but not all, of the decisions whether to prosecute in the area of pornography, has no responsibility for the state of the law. That responsibility is borne by his colleague, the Home Secretary. The Home Secretary is subject to different influences and pressures and has his own sets of values and priorities. To ask the Home Secretary for legislation before a sound basis for reform of the law had been ascertained would have been both foolish and unproductive. My request therefore was for a wide-ranging inquiry by an objective and widely representative group. Eventually the request was granted and Mr Merlyn Rees established the Committee under the distinguished and far-sighted chairmanship of Professor Bernard Williams. Its members could hardly be faulted for objectivity, concern and good sense.

Professor Simpson's most interesting account traces the events which led up to and followed the establishment of what was virtually a Royal Commission in character, if not in title. He describes the method and manner of its proceedings, the gradual formation of its views based on the weight of evidence rather than on pre-conceived opinions and the way in which its excellent report was compiled. His work would be of value if it did no more than portray the process by which a number of separate individuals from varying disciplines achieved a unity and produced a consensus which led to a remarkable unanimity. But Professor Simpson goes further. He takes up the story from the publication of the report, surveys the history – or unhappily lack of history – of what followed and then looks back at the report with the benefit of hindsight.

It is too frequently the fate of august reporting bodies that their reports lie for years in Whitehall pigeon-holes because they are thought to be too hot for Ministers to handle. Cynics indeed advise that Ministers should only establish Committees of Inquiry to enable their own views to be reproduced in the reports so as to provide them with objective backing. In the case of the Williams Committee there was neither such motive nor such consequence. It was indeed a scandal that it took a Private Member's Bill touching upon a small part of the Committee's area of investigation to produce any discussion at all of the report in the House of Commons.

Mr Timothy Sainsbury's Indecent Displays Bill was an honest attempt to deal with what might be called the environmental aspect of pornography. Unfortunately, by making his context that of indecency Mr Sainsbury greatly limited the scope of his Bill. However, it broadly represented the thinking of Mr Sainsbury's party and, having the Home Secretary's support, passed through Parliament despite a good deal of criticism, mainly of its limited approach. The Government gave teeth to the intended environmental protection in its own subsequent legislation which gave local authorities power, in their complete discretion, to forbid or permit the establishment of "sex shops". The controversy over this legislation arose from the belief of some that Parliament ought not to be seen to sanction such doubtful establishments, it being assumed that a "sex shop" is the starting-point for original sin. Both Bills are now law; and it will be interesting to tread the streets of Soho in a year or two's time to see whether its character has materially changed for the better. But whatever their effect on the visual displays of Soho, neither piece of legislation goes to the root of the problems resulting from the quagmire of pornography laws.

It would have been too much to hope for a unanimous welcome for a report as liberal as Williams, notwithstanding that it deployed in persuasive and readable language the unanimous view of a distinguished and disparate group of citizens. It was in particular forseeable that it would be attacked by those who had always been convinced that pornography depraves and corrupts and who therefore found disturbing the conclusion by Williams that the objective evidence did not give credence to that view. But those who read the report objectively could hardly fail to be persuaded that, if anything, the Committee was over-cautious in its conclusion that a link between pornography and sexual or violent crime could not be either established or refuted. The evidence seemed to point strongly to a lack of connection and to establish that the problem is one of taste rather than of moral welfare.

In looking back at the report after an interval of years Professor Simpson is able to display the same objectivity as the Committee evidently showed towards their task. He accepts some part of the criticism; the report was perhaps not in all respects completely logical. But with a subject so riddled with anomalies it would be remarkable to find a report which in no respect sacrificed logic to the pragmatic requirements of public opinion.

If this interesting book does nothing more, I hope that it will once again exhume the spirit of 'Williams' so that it may continue to haunt whatever Government may be in office. For there may in the future be a Home Secretary sufficiently liberal-minded to look upon the report as the backing he requires for the reform of the whole area of pornography. Until then we must unhappily be content with tinkering around the periphery.

S. C. Silkin QC
Her Majesty's Attorney-General 1974–1979

Contents

Chapter 1

The Appointment of the Williams Committee

The Home Office Committee on Obscenity and Film Censorship was formally established on 13 July 1977, under the chairmanship of Bernard Williams, then Professor of Philosophy in Cambridge and Provost of King's College. Its terms of reference were "to review the laws governing obscenity, indecency and violence in publications, displays and entertainments in England and Wales, except in the field of broadcasting, and to review the arrangements for film censorship in England and Wales; and to make recommendations". The Home Secretary at the time was Mr. Merlyn Rees, but the formal announcement of the government's intention to appoint a committee with "broadly based membership" had been made by Lord Harris, Minister of State at the Home Office, in a debate on the Criminal Law Bill in the House of Lords on 14 December of the previous year, and the Attorney-General had earlier in the year indicated that a decision to set up a committee had been taken. The Bill, which later became the Criminal Law Act 1977, modified the law relating to the crime of conspiracy, but retained the much criticised common law offences of conspiracy to corrupt public morals and conspiracy to outrage public decency. The law on these offences had been considered both by the Law Commission and by a Home Office Working Party on Vagrancy and Street Offences, but the Home Office view was that what was required before new legislation was introduced was "a fundamental review of the laws in the field of obscenity, indecency and censorship".

Responsibility for the administration and content of the general criminal law is in many countries the responsibility of a single government department, a Ministry of Justice. Here it is shared uneasily between the Lord Chancellor's Department, the Home Office and the Law Officers (with the Director of Public Prosecutions under them), the latter being particularly concerned with the actual enforcement of the law.

The Attorney-General of the time, Mr. Samuel Silkin, and his colleague, the Solicitor-General, were continually presented with the problems of working with the existing laws on pornography, and therefore conscious of their defects: I understand that it was pressure from them which encouraged the Home Office to become involved in investigating a possible wholesale revision of the law.

Hence the appointment of the Williams Committee, though the exclusion of broadcasting from its terms of reference deprived it of any chance to survey the whole field; broadcasting had already been entrusted to a committee chaired by Lord Annan, which reported in February of 1977, before the Williams Committee started its work. The archaic crime of blasphemy also lay outside its terms of reference: at the time it was appointed this crime was generally thought to have become, for all practical purposes, extinct.

It is idle to speculate on the internal discussions within the Home Office which gave rise to "the Home Office view" except to say that the highly controversial nature of the subject led, in all probability, to the decision not to entrust the review to the two regular bodies concerned with the reform of criminal law – the Law Commission and the Criminal Law Revision Committee. Both bodies are dominated by senior practising lawyers, and in the case of the latter, criminal lawyers, and it was in all probability thought that neither would, because of their composition, be capable of producing a report which would inspire any confidence outside the legal profession. They are also of course predominantly male; recently the Criminal Law Revision Committee, considering sexual offences, consisted, believe it or not, of sixteen men and one woman. Certainly the composition of the Williams Committee, which included amongst its thirteen members only two professional lawyers (an Old Bailey judge, John Leonard, and a solicitor, Ben Hooberman) must be taken to reflect some clear decision on the character of the committee within the Home Office, and though it was predominantly male it had *three* women! Thirteen is a favourite Home Office number, which no doubt the late Margaret Murray would have explained as a survival of the old religion, but we included, as far as I am aware, no witches. The other members were David Robinson, Times film critic, Richard Mathews, former Chief Constable of Warwickshire, Vivian White, Secretary of the United Carribean Association and a youth and community worker in Cardiff, John Weightman, a professor of French at Westfield College, the Right Reverend John Tinsley, Bishop of Bristol, Dr. Anthony Storr, a consultant psychotherapist, Sheila Rothwell of the Equal Opportunities Committee, Polly Toynbee, journalist, and Jessie Taylor, a headmistress from Manchester.

Previous Reviews of the Law

Despite its non-legal character, the primary concern of the Williams Committee was with "the laws", and the laws in question ranged well outside the criminal law. We need a term for this subject matter, and I shall use the term pornography, meaning, roughly, material whose function is to sexually arouse, and whose content infringes conventions of decency in sexual matters. In 1977, and the position today is worse, these laws constituted a chaotic rag-bag of cases and statutes. The former dated back to the entertaining case of **R.** v **Sedley** in 1663, and the latter to the Vagrancy Act of 1824. It would be tedious to review all this material; this is done in the Williams Report. From time to time, committees and commissions of one kind or another had reviewed either the whole area, or parts of it, but had achieved little success in generating any general tidying up of the law. The earliest such body was the early nineteenth century Criminal Law Commission. In its sixth report, published in 1841, it recommended that the criminal law ought only to restrain publications tending either to a breach of the peace, or those "which tend to the subversion of religion, or, in general, to the destruction of the principles of virtue and morality, which are essential to good conduct, order and decency". Their seventh report contained a draft of suitable legislation, but Parliament did not act upon it. In this century, aspects of the field have been reviewed on a number of occasions. In 1908, a Joint Select Committee of both Houses of Parliament investigated "lotteries and indecent advertisements", and in their Report recommended a comprehensive reform of the law; a bill was even drafted, but never introduced. More recently, a Departmental Committee on Children and the Cinema, under the chairmanship of the late K.C. Wheare, worked on the subject between 1948 and 1950, succeeded by a Select Committee of the House of Commons on Obscene Publications (1957–8), a Select Committee of both Houses of Parliament on Censorship of the Theatre (1966–67), the Law Commission (1973–6) and a Home Office Working Party on Vagrancy and Street Offences (1971–6). Though concerned with a different subject matter, the Wolfenden Committee on Homosexual Offences and Prostitution (1954–57) also became involved with related issues of general legislative principle, and there have also been unofficial enquiries, such as those organised by the Arts Council (1968–9), the Conservative lawyers (1971) and by Lord Longford (1971–2) and a group of fifty three individuals (of whom forty-six signed the report) with the support of the Dulverton Trust. The consequence of all this activity had not however been a simplified but rather a more involved body of law, and the appointment of the Williams Committee provided therefore an opportunity to prepare a comprehensive scheme for the general reform of the law falling within its terms of reference.

The Principal Areas of Legal Control

What then were the principal laws in force in 1977 in relation to obscenity, pornography and indecency? Now any law which is technically in force *may* be put into effect: a modern example of this fact is the resurrection in 1978 in **R** v **Lemon and Gay News** of the offence of blasphemy, described back in 1979 by Lord Denning as "a dead letter", and last previously used back in 1922 in **R** v **Gott.** But by the 1970s there existed three areas in which legal controls regularly operated, each one governed by different bodies of law. Publications (whether consisting of text or pictures or a combination of the two) fell under the provisions of the Obscene Publications Act of 1959, amended in minor details in 1964. Customs control over the importation of "indecent or obscene prints, paintings, photographs, books, cards, lithographic or other engravings, or any other indecent or obscene articles" was based on Acts of 1876 and 1952. The commercial cinema was regulated by a system of prior censorship developed out of legislation of 1909 and 1952. Each of these areas requires separate consideration, before we pass on to an account of other areas in which control could be exercised, and to an account also of the less commonly employed legal provisions.

The Obscene Publications Acts 1959 and 1964

The Obscene Publications Act of 1959 represented an attempt to compromise between the policy of suppressing pornography and obscenity on the one hand, and protecting art and literature on the other. Before 1959, control over publications had depended upon the use of the common law crime of publishing an obscene "libel", an offence first invented by the judges back in 1727. A definition of this offence – that is to say a form of words describing the offence which could be used by magistrates and juries – was not fully developed until 1868, when, in **R** v **Hicklin**, Chief Justice Cockburn said:

"I think the test of obscenity is this, whether the tendency of the matter charged as obscenity is to deprave and corrupt those whose minds are open to such immoral influences and into whose hands a publication of this sort may fall".

Though the definition of obscenity was not the issue in this case, the Hicklin definition, which is probably derived directly or indirectly from the ideas of the early utilitarians, came to be accepted, and a slightly modified version of it was enacted in the Act of 1959. But the operation of the pre-1959 common law of obscene libel, based on the "deprave and corrupt" definition, had attracted criticism in the 1950s from the Society of Authors and others on the ground that it operated unfairly and inappropriately when used against work of literary or artistic merit, a complaint reinforced by prosecutions brought in 1954 against Secker and Warburg, THE PHILANDERER, Heinemann, THE IMAGE AND THE SEARCH and Hutchinson, SEPTEMBER IN QUINZE. The law, it was argued, was defective in not requiring the court to consider works of literature as a whole, in restricting what was lawful to books appropriate for children, and in making no provision for a defence based on literary, artistic or other social merit, supported by appropriate expert evidence. Out of all this came the modified definition of obscenity in the Act of 1959, and the new statutory defence which has come to be called the public good defence. An article is in law obscene under the Act if:

"its effect or (where the article comprises two or more distinct items) the effect of any one of its items is, if taken as a whole, such as to tend to deprave and corrupt persons who are likely, having regard to all relevant circumstances, to read, see or hear the matter contained as embodied in it".

This, it will be noted, departs from the common law in requiring the 'item' to be considered as a whole, and does not define obscenity simply in terms of those into whose hands the material *may* fall. But, the Act goes on, no conviction should follow:

"if it is proved that publication of the article in question is justified as being for the public good on the grounds that it is in the interests of science, literature, art or learning or of other objects of general concern".

Expert evidence was made admissible on the 'public good' defence, though such evidence is not admissible on the question of obscenity itself; 'expert' however is not defined. The 'public good' defence carried out one of the declared objects of the 1959 Act: "to provide for the protection of literature". Its first great airing took place in the LADY CHATTERLEY case in 1960, but the acquittal in that and other cases may be either because the work is not thought obscene, or because its publication is in the public good. The jury does not specify.

Another declared object was "to strengthen the law concerning pornography", and the procedures provided under the Act expressed this object. The Act by section two thus created an offence of publishing an obscene article which was triable either summarily by magistrates (but only with the accused's consent) or on indictment before a jury (now in the Crown Court). A prosecution under section two, with its right to jury trial, was thought appropriate where the accused proposed to contest the charge of obscenity or, more particularly, raise the defence of "public good"; here jury trial seems appropriate. A different procedure, set out in section three, involves forfeiture. Material may be seized under warrant and submitted to a magistrates' court, which may order its destruction. This involves no charge of crime against any individual, though provision was made enabling the owner of the material, or other interested persons, to contest the procedure and defend the articles, if they wish to do so. This form of proceeding was designed to provide an effective and fairly summary means of suppressing obviously illegal material, and dates back to an Act of 1857, introduced by Lord Campbell, the then Chief Justice; the technique is borrowed from customs legislation. The dual system of procedure, if it was to work as intended, required the use of section two proceedings whenever any question of artistic or other merit was in issue, and back in 1959 it seems to have been thought that the distinction between straightforward filth (suitable for forfeiture proceedings) and works of possible merit (suitable for criminal prosecution) would present no difficulty to the prosecuting authorities; a prevailing error in this field is the belief that although obscenity is hard to define we can all agree on what it is if confronted with it: the elephant fallacy. The Obscene Publications Act of 1964 was merely an amending Act, and did not modify the basic scheme of the 1959 Act. Thus photographic negatives were not covered by the 1959 Act, and this was remedied; a technical problem over the definition of "publication" was dealt with, and other minor changes were made.

A curious defect in the scheme of the 1959 and 1964 Acts is that no legal right for a publisher to insist on jury trial is built into the forfeiture procedure provided by section three of the 1959 Act. Argument as to whether the article is obscene or not, or whether it is protected by the public good defence *can* be raised before magistrates, but the spirit of the legislation was to allow such matters to be aired before a jury if a publisher wished seriously to contest these matters. In the debate on the 1964 Act, Mr. Roy Jenkins attempted to build a right of jury trial into section three, but his amendment was withdrawn when the Law Officers gave an undertaking to respect the spirit of the legislation. The undertaking, given by Sir Peter Rawlinson, the then Solicitor General, was in effect that if a publisher made it clear that he would not accept an adverse result in a forfeiture proceeding, and persist in publishing, the Crown would then take proceedings under section two by prosecution, thus giving the publisher the opportunity to put his case to a jury. The precise scope of this undertaking has been a source of controversy, and its practical working very unsatisfactory. One of the problems is that a publisher is not necessarily informed or consulted at all before forfeiture proceedings are taken against the stock of a local retailer; he may never hear of them at all. Another problem is that the text of the original undertaking envisaged attention to the views of the publisher, but did not cater for the fact that an author might legitimately want a jury to be involved before his books were ordered to be destroyed.

Certain features of the regime of the Obscene Publications Acts are perhaps curious. The first is that the offence created by section two of the Act of 1959 is not limited to commercial publication for gain; the definition of "publishing" is wide, and, for example, includes giving or lending an obscene article. The second is that the definition of "article" is very wide too, going well beyond what would normally be called a publication. In particular it includes all forms of film or recording, including a video-recording. The third is that the definition of obscenity is contextual – publication of the same article may be obscene in one context and not in others. Neither under proceedings by prosecution nor by forfeiture is a particular article – say a book – judicially branded as obscene, nor is it officially declared legal by an acquittal. i.e. it may be obscene in one context and not in another. The fourth is that whilst private individuals may in general prosecute under section 2, only "official" proceedings by the police or Director of Public Prosecutions were permitted for forfeiture under section 3. This enabled the Director to ensure that the spirit of the legislation was observed.

The courts have to interpret Acts of Parliament and explain them to juries, and over the Obscene Publications Act they got themselves into a terrible muddle. After considerable dithering they came in time to say that an individual was 'corrupted' if he indulged in sexual fantasies and no more; the purity of the mind was the principal object of the law, Lord Wilberforce assured us in the leading case of **D.P.P.** v **Whyte** in 1972. Any old sexual fantasies, so Lord Pearson ruled, would do; they need not include any originality or abnormality. Lurking behind all this is no doubt the old horror of masturbation, though the case law has never openly said so, so strong is the taboo even today on mentioning the practice. Decisions emphasised that under the Act the test is not the offensiveness of the material, but, quite inconsistently, judges have often in directing juries invited them to bear in mind contemporary acceptable standards of decent people. In reality therefore obscenity as a concept under the Obscene Publications Act has become a mixed idea; essentially juries are invited to rule on whether the material is a socially acceptable form of pornography or not, and acceptablility here turns upon the degree to which it violates concepts of decency and decorum. Of course much erotic material, such as romantic novelettes, is accepted by society. There is legal authority for extending the concept of obscenity to non-pornographic material, but this has had little effect.

Customs Control

For the purposes of import control, the Customs Consolidation Act of 1876, which is still in force, employed a different definition of goods which may not be imported: ***"indecent or obscene*** *prints, paintings, photographs, books, cards, lithographic or other engravings, or any other indecent articles"*. This provision originated in a Customs Act of

1846, and thus pre-dates the definition of obscenity in the Hicklin case of 1868, which has never been applied to customs legislation. This, together with the use of the weaker alternative concept of "indecency" makes the law governing what may be imported more rigorous than the law governing internal circulation: a cynic might say that the legislation served to protect the home product. The procedures available under the Act of 1876 and the Customs and Excise Management Act of 1979 provided both for forfeiture proceedings (similar to those first applied to internal distribution by the Act of 1857 and now by the Obscene Publications Act of 1959), and for criminal prosecution in the case of deliberate violation of the prohibition on imports. Customs legislation, however, confers very much more draconian powers on the authorities than the Obscene Publications Acts; for example, a car carrying pornography is itself liable to forfeiture. These draconian powers serve to give the Customs and Excise wide discretionary powers of punishment, untrammelled by any restraint by the rule of law, though there was no evidence presented to the Williams Committee suggesting official abuse of these powers. Customs seizure of pornography is rarely contested. Commercial films largely enter the country by air, and can be and are sometimes seized by Customs Officers in advance of any showing in this country.

The Censorship of Films

The legal controls embodied in the Obscene Publications Acts and Customs legislation do not involve any element of inspection and censorship *before* distribution, nor do they embody any mechanism which effectively licenses or legitimizes a publication as being within the law, though of course import controls do involve seizure before distribution in the United Kingdom. In the case of the commercial cinema, however, an elaborate and strange system of prior-censorship had been developed by the film industry and the local authorities under the aegis of the Home Office. This system originated in the Cinematograph Act of 1909, passed *"to safeguard the public from the danger which arises from fires at cinematograph entertainments"*. Local authorities were, on safety grounds, given the power to license cinemas and attach conditions to such licences. In a case in 1911 the High Court upheld the attachment of conditions relating to matters other than safety. Confronted with complaints as to the character of certain films, the industry established its own classifying and censoring body, The British Board of Film Censors. In 1913, (and with the blessing of the Home Office), the practice developed of local authorities accepting the decisions of the Board and licensing cinemas on the condition that they conformed to the Board's decisions. The board operated its now traditional softly softly catchee monkey system of social? regulation. The legislation of 1909 only covered inflammable film, but the Cinematograph Act of 1952 extended the licensing power to cover non-inflammable film and indeed shows produced by other techniques; it also *required* licensing authorities to impose conditions excluding children from "unsuitable" films, without producing any test of suitability. The licensing authorities – now district councils or the Greater London Council – in general had come to accept a set of model conditions devised by the Home Office, though the Greater London Council used a slightly different set. The principal model condition was that:

no film, other than a current newsreel, shall be exhibited unless it received a certificate of the British Board of Film Censors or is the subject of the licensing authority's permission.

This made the licensing authority a possible appeal court from the Board, and authorities could refuse to permit the showing of films approved by the Board, or vary their classification. Some authorities did adopt an active "go it alone" policy; most had come to adopt a policy of keeping out of direct involvement in censorship. The Greater London Council licensing conditions in force when the Williams Committee was set up specifically banned films (whether or not approved by the Board) which were:

1 (a) likely to encourage or to invite crime; or
(b) to lead to disorder; or
(c) to stir up hatred against any section of the public in Great Britain on grounds of colour, race or ethnic or national origins; or
2 the effects of which are, if taken as a whole, such as to tend to deprave and corrupt persons who are likely to see it, or
3 which contain a grossly indecent performance thereby outraging standards of public decency.

The last condition had been added because in 1976, the Court of Appeal ruled (in **R.** v **G.L.C. ex parte Blackburn**) that cinema licensing authorities, whether adopting the certificates of the British Board, or running their own system, could not organise their arrangements so as to permit the showing of 'unlawful' films, and by a tortuous process of reasoning ruled that the correct test of illegality here was not the common law "corrupt and deprave" formula derived from the Hicklin case and embodied in the Obscene Publications Act (1959) but the common law test of indecency, which, in the words of Lord Reid in an earlier case "includes anything which an ordinary decent man or woman would find to be shocking, disgusting and revolting". Lord Denning indeed thought this test a better weapon:

"For this simple reason: pornography shocks and disgusts decent people, but it does not tend to deprave and corrupt them. They revolt from it and turn away from it."

After the Williams Committee was appointed matters were further complicated by section 53 of the Criminal Law Act of 1977 which came into force on 1 December 1977, and which extended the Obscene Publications Act to film shows. Previously, the Obscene Publications Acts of 1959 and 1964 did not apply to "cinematography exhibitions" (though it did apply to the sale, etc. of films, for example in a shop). Hence the "deprave and corrupt" test, subject to a slightly variant form of "public good" defence modelled on the provisions of the Theatres Act 1968, came to apply to film shows, including film shows in commercial licensed cinemas which observed the B.B.F.C. censorship system. The effect of the 1977 Act was to *substitute* the statutory obscenity test ("deprave and corrupt") for the common law indecency test, not to add a new additional requirement.

Under these elaborate provisions, the only legal recipients of powers of censorship were the district councils and Greater London Council. But with some exceptions, the practice of classification and censorship had largely passed into the hands of the British Board of Film Censors, an institution possessing no statutory basis, and one financed by the film industry itself through fees charged by the Board for viewing and classifying films. In 1977, it classified films as:

"U" – Passed for General exhibition

"A" – Passed for general exhibition, but parents/guardians are advised that the film contains material they might prefer their children not to see

"AA" – Passed as suitable only for exhibition to persons of fourteen and over. When a programme contains an AA film, no person under fourteen may be admitted.

"X" – Passed as suitable only for exhibition to adults. When a programme includes an **X** film, no person under eighteen may be admitted.

(see Appendix B for 1983 classifications)

In addition, there was a further category – no certificate issued. The Board would also advise on cuts which, if made, would give the film a desired certificate, or enable it to obtain a certificate at all, and the Board, by insisting on the removal of a blood spurt or overenthusiastic wiggle of the bottom or whatever, could modify the effect of a scene to which its examiners took exception. The Board possesses a Chairman (in 1977 Lord Harlech), but operated from day to day under the control of its Secretary, Mr. James Ferman, employing a very small technical staff and four anonymous film examiners (one of whom turned out to my amazement to be an ex-pupil of mine). Noteworthy moments in the film provoked a shout from the examiner: the projectionist then thrust a scrap of paper into the reel, thereby identifying it. One of its functions was accepted as being that of ensuring that its granting of certificates conformed to the law. But the law in reality provided the Board with only limited guidance. The Board also had to ensure that its decisions were broadly acceptable to the licensing authorities; if it lost their confidence its very existence would be in the melting pot. They did not *have* to pay any attention to its decisions.

At the top of the scale, where the decision involved is whether to issue a certificate at all, the law does provide tests of illegality, albeit tests which may be problematical to apply. Since 1 December 1976, a film must not "deprave and corrupt" (subject to the public good defence), involve forms of cruelty to certain animals (forbidden by the Cinematograph Films (Animals) Act of 1937), or incite to crime or racial hatred so as to infringe the Race Relations Act of 1976. But a B.B.F.C. certificate in no way *guarantees* that the law has been conformed to, though, in the case of public commercial films (16mm. or above), the legislation of 1977 which brought film shows within the Obscene Publication Acts scheme required the consent of the Director of Public Prosecutions to proceedings. This enabled the Director to treat certificates as guarantees if he wished, and enabled him to exercise some covert influence over the B.B.F.C. So far as children were concerned, the law neither defined appropriate ages, nor explained when films were "unsuitable". Hence, the standards operated by the British Board were largely the creation of its members, in particular its Secretary and Chairman, operating of course in the glare of public opinion, and with the D.P.P. breathing down their necks. Further the Board had always adopted a practice of refusing certificates entirely, or insisting on cuts, on grounds which, whatever their merits, had no basis whatever in law. In the more remote past, some of their practices were highly comic – the refusal, for example, to permit scenes involving

"Subjects dealing with India, in which British officers are seen in an odious light." (1913–1915).

In modern times the Board, whilst continuing to refuse certificates to films which are in no sense unlawful, has been particularly concerned that its certificates be acceptable to licensing authorities. But throughout its history it had to some degree imposed its own standards rather that follow those externally imposed upon it, and in 1977 this remained the position. An extraordinary concentration of power resided in this tiny institution, operating from modest premises in Soho Square.

Enforcement in the Principal Areas of Control

Although subject to both local variations produced by objective conditions (for example, the geographical distribution of pornography shops), and by the policies of different Chief Constables, and subject to extraordinary fluctuations from year to year, the Obscene Publications Acts have been regularly employed in efforts to control pornography. Thus, in 1977, magistrates' courts made 377 orders for forfeiture of obscene articles, and the Metropolitan Police alone seized 375,484 individual items. In the same year, 174 persons were proceeded against, and 141 found guilty, 48 being sentenced to terms of imprisonment (in 32 cases suspended sentences). The Customs service in the same year seized 189,848 indecent or obscene items, and indirectly had some 9,000 overseas postal packets opened. So enforcement was taking place on a significant scale, whatever view might be taken as to its real effectiveness in controlling the trade in pornography. The film censorship system in 1977 gave rise to only a single criminal prosecution under the Cinematograph Act of 1909, but this is in reality an index of its almost complete effectiveness in excluding non-certificated films from the regular commercial public cinemas; distributors, cinema owners and cinema managers co-operated wholeheartedly with the system. Its effectiveness in keeping those well under fourteen (or eighteen) out of cinemas showing **AA** or **X** films was considerable, though there was obviously some leakage at the age margins. But there were and in reality, if not in theory, still are, enormous gaps in the system. Film censorship under the Act of 1952 was not applicable at all to film shows exempted from the legislation and, particularly in London and some other large cities, cinema clubs (some bona fide, others more dubious, formed merely to escape control) fell outside any effective control. Indirectly, of course, customs seizures could restrict what films were easily available, a form of pre-censorship so far as the home market was concerned. Sales of pornographic movies could be caught too by the Obscene Publications Acts, but its procedures did not involve any system of prior censorship, and in general the enforcement of the law was so patchy and unenthusiastic that it appeared to have little real effect on what was available to seekers after pornography. No doubt it put up the price, and the pornographer discounted the risks inherent in their trade, much as any commercial undertaking will do.

Other Legal Controls

Though relatively unimportant in the sense of being used less frequently, there existed a considerable number of other legal provisions which could be used to control pornography, obscenity and indecency.

Indecent exhibitions and displays could give rise to criminal proceedings under the Vagrancy Acts 1824 and 1838, in London under the Metropolitan Police Act 1839, in other cities by the Town Police Clauses Act of 1847, which created an offence of offering for sale or exhibiting "any profane, indecent, or obscene Book, Paper, Print, Drawing, Painting or Representation, or sings any profane or obscene Song or Ballad, or uses any profane or obscene language". In 1977, proceedings were taken against nineteen individuals, one of whom was even imprisoned. **Indecent advertisements** were principally covered by the Indecent Advertisements Act 1889, which covers the public display of indecent or obscene advertising matter: the legislation also covers displays and exhibitions generally. A mere four persons were proceeded against under this Act in 1977. The **postal service** was regulated by the Post Office Act of 1953, which prohibits the sending of "indecent or obscene" material through the post, and by the **Unsolicited Goods and Services Act** 1971, which extends beyond indecent or obscene matter to any unsolicited material "which describes or illustrates human sexual techniques". Some 9,000 packages originating from overseas were opened and seized in 1977

as an aspect of Customs control; very few seizures took place of packages originating in England and Wales, and no figures exist for the very occasional action against unsolicited sexual material. **Theatrical performances** were covered by the Theatres Act 1968, which replaced a system of pre-censorship by the Lord Chamberlain with provisions very similar to but not identical to the Obscene Publications Act, based upon a "tendency to deprave and corrupt" definition of obscenity. The Act embodies a "public good" defence. Proceedings under the Theatres Act required the consent of the Attorney General, and proceedings had only once been instituted since the Act was passed. **Children** were specially protected from "Horror Comics" by the Children and Young Persons (Harmful Publications) Act 1955, which covers material portraying or describing:
(a) the commission of crimes; or
(b) acts of violence or cruelty; or
(c) incidents of a repulsive or horrible nature; in such a way that the work as a whole would tend to corrupt a child or young person into whose hands it might fall'.
(Customs control provided a further protection in this context.)

In addition to this battery of legislation, there were common law offences which could be used by enthusiasts to control pornography – the principal such offences existing in 1977 were "conspiracy to corrupt public morals" or "outrage public decency," and the offence of "keeping a disorderly house". These offences could be used to embrace conduct falling outside the scope of any of the statutory offences relating to pornography, and the common law did not recognise any specific defence based upon ideas of public good or artistic merit. Prosecutions were however rare – in 1977 nobody was proceeded against for conspiracy to corrupt public morals, the last prosecution having taken place back in 1975. But the possibility remained. Blasphemy constituted another offence which could be charged, and in 1976 a prosecution was brought over a bad poem "The Love that Dares to Speak Its Name" by one James Kirkup accompanied by a bad drawing in the style of Beardsley. The essence of this offence lies in the offensiveness of the material, not in its supposed tendency to corrupt, or encourage others in sin or whatever.

Official Control over Prosecutions

As a general rule any individual can initiate a criminal prosecution, though of course the vast majority of prosecutions are initiated by the police. There existed (and still exist) many exceptions to this, and in the case of laws relating to pornography the position in 1977 was complex. Private prosecutions were possible under the Obscene Publications Act except in the case of film shows using 16mm. film or above, under the Post Office Act, under the 19th century legislation governing indecent displays, and for common law offences. Otherwise some form of official consent was required – thus the Attorney General had to consent to proceedings under the Theatres' Act, the Director of Public Prosecutions to proceedings under the Protection of Children Act, the Commissioner of Customs and Excise to proceedings under the Customs Act. Needless to say, no clear principle lay behind these rules, which had become law at varying periods.

The Confused State of the Law

It will be obvious from this very much simplified summary of the State of the Law in 1977 that there existed no shortage of laws relating to pornography and indecency, but rather an *'embarras de richesses'*– a disorderly body of laws made at very different times and lacking any apparent consistency. Thus some laws employed a special concept of *obscenity* defined in terms of a "tendency to corrupt and deprave" – this was the position under the Obscene Publications Act and the Theatres Act. Other laws relied on variants of a two-pronged definition of the prescribed material – it must be "indecent *or* obscene", and here, as under Customs legislation, "obscenity" was not, according to the case law, defined in terms of a "tendency to corrupt and deprave"; it bore merely its dictionary sense, whatever that might seem to be. Commercial chain cinemas were governed by an effective system of pre-censorship, depending in part upon the practice of a private organisation, the British Board of Film Censors; theatrical performances and exhibitions were not. Under the Theatres Act and Obscene Publications Acts the artistic or other *merit* of the play or publication could be ventilated in court under a public good defence, presented with the assistance of "expert" witnesses; no such provisions protected the commercial cinema. Widely different penalties applied – an indecent exhibition under the Vagrancy Act of 1824 could attract a prison sentence of three months or a fine of £100 (except, incredibly, in February when it was not a leap year; this was altered to £200 after the 1977 Act came into force). Conspiracy to corrupt public morals attracted the grim theoretical possibliity of life imprisonment or fine without limit; an offence under s.2 of the Obscene Publications Act could, if tried on indictment, attract a prison sentence of up to three years and fine without limit. The point need not be laboured – the law was an untidy mess. And it still is, though the mess is now worse. But in order to put the matter in context all English criminal law is more or less in the same condition, and attempts to tidy the law up have, particularly when dominated by senior judges, produced more mess still. This has for example happened over the law of theft, tidied in 1968 and retidied in 1978. It is now in the worst state of confusion ever achieved in English legal history..

Why the Williams Committee?

Some government committees are set up in response to some individual scandal or *cause célèbre,* some outburst of popular or political feeling, or to investigate some urgent and pressing social problem. No single incident provoked the appointment of the Williams Committee. Instead it was set up as part of the general process, always continuing and one fears never completed, of tidying up and rationalising the law (principally the criminal law). But the context in which the government's decision was taken was one in which there existed considerable dissatisfaction with the existing state of control and regulation of pornography. Some critics were primarily concerned with the law, and objected to the form it took and the apparently arbitrary way in which it was enforced. Others were more concerned to criticise what might be called the end product – a society in which real or supposed pornography was too readily, or not sufficiently readily obtainable. Virtually nobody seemed to be pleased with the way things were. How widespread this discontent was is perhaps impossible to tell; no doubt very many people neither knew nor cared what the position was. But this is true of many states of affairs which are viewed by some as social problems, or which regularly feature in the media.

The general background to this dissatisfaction was no doubt the profound changes in public taste and acceptability (or some would say profound corruption of public morals and standards of public decency) associated with the rise of the permissive society in the 1960s and 1970s, and the sharp clash of attitudes between generations which this phenomenon produced. Of course there is nothing new in changes in taste – what was peculiar about this period was the rapidity of change. Accompanying it (and it seems to me idle to argue here about cause and effect) was the vigorous commercial exploitation of a new public market for pornography presented principally in the form of glossy colour magazines, the so-called "adult" or "girlie" magazines such as "Whitehouse", "Rustler" and "Club" at the more extreme end of the market and magazines such as "Men Only" and "Playboy" at the less extreme end. During the same period literary publishers reacted to the changes in taste and to the opportunities presented by the introduction of the "public good" defence in the Act of 1959 to produce works which could not possibly have been published before 1959; the landmark here was Penguin's publication of LADY CHATTERLEY'S LOVER in 1960, and the acquittal of Penguin from a charge under the Obscene Publications Act in November of that year after a sensational trial. During the same period, but most particularly whilst John Trevelyan was its secretary (1959–1972), the British Board of Film Censors reflected (or its critics claimed, led) the movement for relaxing controls over the cinema – here the certification of the romantic LAST TANGO IN PARIS (1974) and the failure, in part for purely technical reasons, of attempts to take private legal proceedings to ban the film under the 1824 Vagrancy Act and the Obscene Publications Acts were viewed at the time as critical. As the regular system of film censorship was relaxed, there also developed a widespread exploitation of the legal exemptions from the system of film censorship. It had never been the case that *all* film shows were regulated – for example, private home movie shows, becoming more common with increased affluence, were never controlled. In particular the Act of 1952 contained a provision exempting film exhibitions:

to which the public are not admitted, or to which the public are admitted without payment

and also exempted certain non-profit making organisations

certified by the Customs and Excise. Under the protection of these provisions the film clubs flourished – some being societies for film buffs; some being genuine clubs, such as some working men's clubs, whose members particularly enjoyed pornographic entertainment, and others being commercial porno-houses operating through a largely fictitious concept of membership. Particularly in Soho the latter type of institution proliferated, with little attempt at concealment. External advertising indeed commonly overstated the depravity of what was on offer inside, as one might expect.

The Discrediting of the Law

The Report of the Williams Committee characterised the period preceding its appointment as being marked by the retreat of the law, a reatreat culminating in the failure of the attempt, in 1976, to prosecute Johannes Hanau, the publisher of INSIDE LINDA LOVELACE. This book first became generally available in England in 1974, and was a pornographic work particularly concerned with oral and anal sexual intercourse, and with the use of vibrators, contraptions now becoming readily available and selling, one is told, briskly. To an older generation, it seemed quite incredible that such a book could be lawfully sold – the judge who tried the case at the Central Criminal Court whose experience of such matters was obviously limited put it thus:

If this book is not obscene within the definition of the Act ***[The Obscene Publications Act 1959]*** *it might well be difficult to imagine anything that would fall within that category.*

Mr Hanau was defended by John Mortimer and Geoffrey Robertson, who ran the public good defence, calling eight "expert" witnesses; Mrs Whitehouse has unkindly called such defence teams 'Mortimer's circus'. These included Anna Coote (journalist), Johnny Speight (actor), Marion Boyars (Publisher) and Dr. Brian Richards, who conceded that some of Miss Lovelace's activities, if not harmful to morals, could actually kill readers attempting to emulate them. The trial was pervaded by deep unreality, it being supposed that the book, which was ghosted, was a sort of genuine diary, which any fool could see it was not. The jury, of nine men and three women, acquitted – whether because they did not think the book would corrupt or deprave, or whether they thought its publication nevertheless in the public good, is unknown. Behind this acquittal lay not only a change in public attitudes, but technical changes in the composition of juries. Since the abolition in 1972 of the property qualification, and in 1971 of the judge's right to exclude women, the composition of juries has altered very significantly, and in particular they had become younger, and less in tune with the ideas of elderly judges.

But perhaps as significant as the retreat of the law has been the discrediting of the law, both in the eyes of those who would seek stronger controls over pornography and those who would prefer the controls to be weakened or abolished. This process was initiated immediately after the passing of the Act of 1959 by the ludicrous case of **R v Penguin Books Ltd.** arising out of the publication of D.H. Lawrence's LADY CHATTERLEY'S LOVER. To have selected for prosecution a company of such high reputation and that for publishing a work by one of the leading literary figures of this century was idiotic enough, but to have entrusted the prosecution to the hands of a legal neanderthal, Mervyn Griffith Jones, guaranteed a fiasco. The defence, handled by Gerald Gardiner, called no less than thirty-five "expert" witnesses to pronounce upon the artistic, literary and even ethical merits of the book. They included leading literary figures – E.M. Forster, Dame Rebecca West, Helen Gardner, publishers – Sir Stanley Unwin, not to mention Sir Allen Lane himself – and a motley array of clerics, academics, critics, as well as Roy Jenkins and Norman St. John Stevas, who had been involved in the passing of the Act. No "experts" were called by the prosecution, though I recall at the time the failure of an attempt to rustle up a few in Oxford, where the proceedings were I recall viewed as pure farce. After a trial lasting six days, the jury acquitted – whether because they found the book was not obscene at all or whether they thought its obscenity was counterbalanced by its literary or ethical merits, or because they were bored with the whole business, did not transpire. The trial was very fully reported and much enjoyed, producing as it did moments of high comedy. The judge who tried the case, Mr. Justice Byrne, was said to have been so astonished by the acquittal that he resigned shortly afterwards. He was, as Christopher Hill once said of Chief Justice Coke, a lawyer and not an intellectual. The absurdity of the case was heightened when the Warden of All Souls, John Sparrow, an expert on these literary matters, revealed that the novel included references to buggery, which Griffith Jones had coyly passed over.

In a sense, it is true, the Lady Chatterley case delivered precisely what the authors of the Act of 1959 wanted – the freeing of literature. But the very fact of the prosecution and its utterly philistine character discredited the prosecuting authorities in their eyes; and the form of the trial, with the pundits pontificating as "experts" on the merits of the work, (offering the received truth of the intelligentsia, in terms appropriate to some weird seminar) discredited the trial as a forum for debate on such questions. To those who sought stronger laws, the verdict was an outrage. Lord Teviot in the Lords called on the government to:

take such steps as are possible to ban for all times writings of this nature, particularly those of the author of this book.

Many found the trial simply comic, and the law in consequence ridiculous.

Since the Lady Chatterley case the process of discrediting the law and its administration has continued. Those who seek stronger and more severe legal controls have kept up a constant barrage of criticism against the police, the prosecuting authorities, the British Board of Film Censors, the law itself in the abstract, and particular lawyers and judges. The "Oz" trial in 1971, which occupied twenty-seven days and dragged on to nearly six weeks, and ended, on appeal, with an acquittal on the obscenity charge, further united hawks and doves in contempt of the law. To Mrs. Whitehouse, the outcome was a disaster; to the New Law Journal, the trial itself was a disaster, and to the public generally the proceedings, a sort of *reductio ad absurdum* of of what had happened in the Lady Chatterley Case, provided prolonged entertainment, the proceedings being handled with real flair by Judge Michael Argyle, who, aided and abetted by such "expert" witnesses as the late Marty Feldman, ensured that comic interest would be maintained. Criticism of the law and its administration has at times been expressed in legal action, as when, in 1972, Mr. Raymond Blackburn brought proceedings in the High Court to compel the Metropolitan Police Commissioner to enforce the law against pornography. Although he failed to get an order, the Court of Appeal expressed considerable sympathy with his claim, and thereafter judges began to join in the process of discrediting the law, by saying that it was in a very defective state; they have continued to say so ever since. In fact, the Metropolitan Police's "Dirty Squad" was then engaged in actually running the pornography business, and the revelation of this further discredited the system. The lack of any control over public indecency was apparent to any visitor to Soho, and numerous attempts, all unsuccessful, were made to strengthen the law. Those who favoured less stringent controls agreed that the existing laws had become more or less unworkable, and added other criticisms which too served to discredit the law – for example, some objected to the activities of the British Board of Film Censors, as stifling the development of the cinema as art. From all sides of the debate there emerged a near unanimity of dissatisfaction with the law and its administration.

Chapter 2

The Work of the Williams Committee

The Committee met for the first time on Friday, 2nd September, 1977, and, thirty-five meetings later, for the last on Wednesday, 31st October, 1979 for the formal signing of the report, which was, almost incredibly, unanimous. Subsequently, some of its members attended a private and entirely respectable party when the report was republished in an abridged form by the Cambridge University Press; otherwise we parted as one might at the end of a long sea-voyage. Our association produced no marriages, divorces, or any other dramatic incidents. The report remains our only achievement, and cost the nation just under £100,000, £38,692 being the cost of printing – how much has been recovered in sales, I have no idea. Committee members are not paid; the costs involved cover their expenses and the expenses of the secretariat. Most of our meetings took place in London, but we spent weekends together, one in a leaky and run-down hotel in Hastings, said to be owned by the Kray family, and the other more elegantly in King's College, Cambridge. Groups from the committee paid the obligatory visit to Denmark, though we were careful to avoid the embarrassing scenes which took place during Lord Longford's visit back in 1971, when indelicate advances were made to the crusading peer "by a 'lady' who appeared afterwards to have been a man"; the intense respectability of Copenhagen assorted oddly with its reputation as the porn capital of Europe, though it did boast a sex shop retailing vibrating caterpillars; catering for some peculiar Scandinavian proclivity. Another group visited Paris; there were trips to Soho and to some of the entertainments provided there, though to avoid publicity we did not descent *en masse,* armed with notepads, at strip joints or porno movie houses. In addition to attending meetings, members of the committee were presented with a massive amount of homework, in the form of reading material circulated postally by the secretariat (none of it, I hasten to add, pornographic). A great deal of time was involved, especially for the Chairman and to a much lesser degree his deputy, who of course had additional meetings to attend and work to prepare.

Our first meeting was a nervous affair, initiated by our being set upon by what seemed to be an endless chain of press photographers – I think only THE LADY and TIMES actually published grim group photographs. As Polly Toynbee later wrote:

No-one was anxious to give away personal first thoughts on the subject, everyone extremely keen to sus out where the others stood. Were we divided between rabid Whitehousians and ferocious free thinkers? Had some departmental thought police been over our likely views and pigeon-holed us a headmistress, a bishop, a policeman, a barrister, a bus driver, three professors, and others?

How quite we were selected remains a mystery. It was rumoured that the Archbishop had been given the nomination of a cleric – hence the selection of the Bishop of Bristol, John Tinsley. Bernard Williams had previously served on a number of similar bodies – the Public Schools Commission (1965–70), the Royal Commission on Gambling (1976–8). I had previously been on a curious **Advisory Group on Rape**, and was rumoured amongst friends to hang around Queen Anne's Gate in a dirty mackintosh in order to secure appointment to committees on sordid subjects. Two members had previously publicly exhibited some mild interest in our subject matter – the chairman Bernard Williams and the psychiatrist, Anthony Storr, had both publicly defended the publication of Hubert Selby's LAST EXIT TO BROOKLYN, published in 1966 by Calder and Boyars who were prosecuted at the Old Bailey in 1967. Calder and Boyars were in fact convicted, but the conviction was quashed by the Court of Appeal in the leading case of **R** v **Calder and Boyars**, essentially upon the ground that the defence case was never adequately presented to the jury in the summing up, a moral as well as a technical victory, particularly since this was the last attempt to prosecute a work of literature under the Obscene Publications Acts. No doubt as film critic of the Times, David Robinson possessed a professional interest in the workings of film censorship; otherwise no members of the committee had exhibited any particular interest in the subject. The appointment of Bernard Williams was the subject of some protest at the time both from the Festival of Light, on the ground that he was not a believing Christian, and a group of peers and MPs, but the rest of us were not similarly honoured. The Home Office is said to keep a special list of "ordinary people" to leaven committees; which of us figure in it I do not know.

The Procedure Followed by the Committee

At our first meeting we were principally concerned to work out an approximate timetable and terminus to our work. We agreed to aim to produce one final public document, a comprehensive report and set of recommendations, and this by the summer of 1979, not a set of working papers. We also agreed to start the tedious and at times extremely disagreeable process of familiarising ourselves with pornography, both that currently obtainable and some from the past, illustrative of the changes in attitudes which had occurred, particularly since the legislation of 1959. Both the Home Office and other official agencies, such as the office of the Director of Public Prosecutions, possess extensive collections of pornographic material which has been seized or used as exhibits, and of course certain types of pornographic material could be openly bought in London. Transporting this material presents problems to the scrupulous, since it cannot legally be posted; instead it has to be carried in the jaws of old and utterly reliable police dogs, or by aged messengers who have long since lost any interest in matters sexual. An exhibition organised by the secretariat divided material into six categories – examples of 19th century pornography; material, mainly books, involved in *causes célèbres*; examples of material such as vulgar sea-side postcards thought obscene, astonishingly enough, as recently as the 1950s; "horror comics" of the type which led to the 1955 Act; American "bondage" and sado-masochistic material; a range of English magazines from the 1970s, illustrating the shifting limits of what publishers felt they could get away with; a collection of expensive glossy and bizarre Scandinavian material, some emanating from the Color-Climax Corporation, said to produce the most explicit material, the Rolls Royce of porn. This included extremely distasteful sadistic and paedophiliac material. Much of what we considered consisted of illustrated magazines and sets of photographs without text of any kind, and 8mm and 16mm films, whose type is indicated by their suggestive titles – "Lesbian Love Machine", "Little Ones in Love", "Convent of Sin", "Bizarre Tastes" and so forth, mostly voyeurish in basic character, and falling into distinguishable genres – sadistic concentration camp, rubber fetishism, material involving animals, flagellation, painting naked bodies, etcetera. God, they say, made us, but he seems to have had some off days. We also made arrangements – or the secretariat did – to see the British Board of Film Censors at work, and to view or see again a number of films which had been or currently were the subject of controversy or legal proceedings, for example A CLOCKWORK ORANGE, PRETTY BABY, STRAW DOGS, THE STORY OF O, SALÒ, AI NO CORRIDA, as well as numerous examples of films in which cuts had been required by the Board before certification. So far as most of the blatantly pornographic was concerned, these viewing sessions did not cause me personally any particular distress or acute repulsion, (nor I fear any pleasurable emotions) and the dreary humourless reptitiveness of pornography induced boredom more than any other reaction. Some of the more extremely violent films, and those dealing with particularly disagreeable sexual perversions, such as coprophilia or gross abuse of children, did, and, understandably enough, there were limits to the exposure which some committee members, or the group as a whole, could tolerate. I have been asked whether in the course of all this my own level of tolerance altered; I can only say that it did not seem to me to do so. Inevitably acquaintances from time to time exhibited some prurient interest in what was becoming of one's psyche; a cross we all had to bear. A certain amount of "Ho Ho-ing" is inevitable..

Hard and Soft Core Pornography

Commonly, pornography is divided in discussion into "hard core" and "soft", with the assumption that the law should principally be aimed against the hard core material as likely to be more socially harmful. But this classification, and the theory behind it, is too simplistic to be of much value, as is an attempted classification employed by the Director of Public Prosecutions into Grades 1, 2, and 3 (essentially soft, harder, hardest). The theory assumes that the softer material, with presumably much the widest appeal, is the least effective, a very peculiar idea: it is of course in the softer end of the market that large audiences are secured. Study of a wide range of material suggests that although classifications of this type, which depend simply upon an assessment of how extreme or strong the material is, has its uses, it runs into the obvious difficulty that individual assessments vary; what is being assessed is either the level of repulsiveness, or, when material causes any erotic arousal or disturbing interest, individual embarrassment and guilt. The subjective character of porn classification was dramatically illustrated when one noted witness appeared before the committee and amazed its members by instancing a photograph of a naked girl sitting on a football as the most appalling item ever.

However, there are other and perhaps more important ways of classifying pornography. One is to divide it by reference to the specific sexual interest for which it caters – "bondage", "spanking", "rubber fetishism", "bestiality", "paedophilia" and so on. Within a category, for example paedophiliac material, porn may consist of very extreme material depicting gross abuse of children, or very mild material, such as photographs of normally clad young girls or boys; material catering for a taste for bestiality, or whatever, may similarly extend over a great range. Another way of classifying porn is to divide by reference to the immediacy of its impact, which depends primarily and very obviously upon the medium involved – filmed violence has a dramatically sharper impact than still photographs; much less has the written word alone. Thus accounts of extreme brutality, for example in the Iliad, or the Bulldog Drummond stories, wholly lack the impact of a film of the same incident. A third is to divide pornography into material which can only be produced by actual cruelty or ill-treatment – some forms of child pornography or bestial material for example fall into this category, but not all.

Out of the experience of studying a large quantity of pornography also came for me at least, and I suspect for other members of the committee, a realisation of greater consciousness of three other important considerations. The first was a numbing awareness of the essentially dreary and rubbishy nature of virtually all pornography, and its profound lack of quality. I recall, for example, the spectacle of the dirty feet of the male performer in one 16mm. film, DATE LINE, which was given over almost entirely to what is called in the trade "humping" and lasted nearly half an hour. The dialogue was confined to the following exchange:

"C'mon kids, let's go to the planetarium."

"No. Over to my place, and have ourselves a ball." followed by prolonged grunting. Presumably the director also became disturbed by the grubby feet, for after a badly concealed cut they appear clean and shining, and the 'humping and grunting proceeded. When any element of artistic pretension is involved, as in the film of THE STORY OF O, porn normally turns into the pseudo art form, 'pornokitsch'. The second consideration was of some bewilderment as to why the weirder material,

which caters for minority interests, is desired at all, let alone (as is the case) purchased by addicts compulsively; the idea that watching the stuff can generate an interest in it which was not latent before is utterly implausible. But on reflection the more repetitive nature of sexual activity, whether "straight" or not, has never reduced its appeal, and the same is no doubt true in the case of deviant tastes. The third consideration was an awareness that when some form of pornography did create aversion (for example, a scene in one unpleasant film which included a supposedly real case of scalping and castration), it was either because it was embarrassing, or shocking, or even physically repellent and nauseating, not because it induced any temptation to imitate. Only on the assumption that members of Home Office committees of thirteen are somehow specially protected by providence, an improbable hypothesis, could our viewing sessions encourage the belief that the principal effect of exposure to pornography was corruption and depravity. And experience confirmed this – no member of the committee then or since, so far as I am aware, took to committing sexual offences, or eating guardsmens' socks, or dressing up in gasmasks. One felt quite safe, even in the Home Office.

The Literature of Pornography

Self-education also involved study of the literature dealing with the legal regulation of pornography, which is very extensive and I fear somewhat repetitive, and with literature dealing with supposed effects. The secretariat produced a select bibliography, listing some forty-four items ranging from the massive report of the U.S. Commission on Obscenity and Pornography, with its nine volumes of technical reports, to ephemera such as Mrs. Whitehouse's WHO DOES SHE THINK SHE IS? Further written material originating within the committee or its secretariat was distributed throughout the life of the committee and classified as "papers"; a total of a hundred and nine such papers were circulated. Early in the life of the committee, such papers were generally simply informative – comprehensive accounts of the existing law, and the working of film censorship, monthly reports of the British Board of Film Censors, surveys of research on the effects of pornography, an article on the historical development of the 'deprave and corrupt' test. Later, as opinion within the committee began to crystallise, they began to include discussion papers dealing with possible schemes for regulation and control, setting out and evaluating different forms a reformed law might take. The industry and efficiency of our secretariat was daunting; any enquiry we made was followed up. For example we were interested in the story, reported by Mrs. Whitehouse, that the Germans had used pornography to soften up the Poles before the 1939 invasion as an act of war. The secretariat duly tracked the source of the story down; it was, as one might expect, a distortion of an account of what happened *after* the fall of Poland. Similarly they tracked down detailed information as to what pornography certain notorious criminals had possessed at the time of their arrest, and indeed followed up an extraordinary range of enquiries for us.

Material originating outside a government committee is called its *evidence*; the term, though hallowed by usage, is a little misleading. It suggests that what is principally involved is factual information, whereas in reality much evidence comprises opinion, assertion and argument. We received written submissions, some (such as that provided by the Festival of Light) very elaborately argued and presented, from just under a hundred and fifty organisations. Some of those submitting evidence were essentially pressure groups – the Campaign for Homosexual Equality, the shadowy National Viewers' and Listeners' Association, the Spare Rib Collective. Some were official or semi-official organisations – the Metropolitan Police, the Justices' Clerks' Society, the Police Federation. Some were professionally concerned – the Criminal Bar Association, the Periodical Publishers Association, W.H. Smith. Some were simply organisations which felt they had something valuable or useful to say – Wanstead Baptist Church, the Girl Guides, the Mothers' Union. As a result of advertisements and press releases, or their own independent initiative, some 1400 individuals wrote us letters, which the secretariat analysed.

Taking Oral Evidence

All this produced a mountain of paper to read, some fascinating and informative, some provocative, much of it repeating standard arguments. All in all, close to two hundred and fifty separate items were involved. At our meetings, however, the major part of the time was devoted to talking to the hundred and twenty-eight individuals who gave oral evidence, and it was in these discussions and the informal talks after them that a committee view began to develop. Those who gave oral evidence included, inevitably, the leading campaigners against pornography – the Earl of Longford, who had to hurry off to lunch with Richard Nixon, a stern moralist and critic of liberal views on pornography, the deeply pessimistic David Holbrook, the vigorous and indeed aggressive litigant, Raymond Blackburn, the crusading Methodist Chief Constable and preacher James Anderton, and of course, Mary Whitehouse herself, clutching her latest shocking piece of pornography from the Danish schools (which, when translated, turned out not to be pornographic at all) ready to do battle with a committee she deeply distrusted. The pornographers we met (too few, I fear), having absorbed the jargon of social work, exuded an air of righteous concern for the welfare of their "clients" and the preservation of high professional standards, whilst the prophets of sexual liberation dreamt, so it seemed, of a world in which not only the lion and the lamb but everyone else would, without inhibitions, lie down together, or, for that matter, stand up together. Some witnesses, most strikingly the representatives of the Customs and Excise, seemed tolerably happy with the state of the law, which their organisation apparently enforces with creditable enthusiasm. One could not but recall the words of the customs officer in Evelyn Waugh's VILE BODIES:

Particularly against books the Home Secretary is. If we can't stamp out literature in the country, we can at least stop it being brought in from outside.

But others professionally close to the law's administration within the country shared a general dissatisfaction with the form it took. Particularly impressive evidence came from some of the central religious organisations, whose representatives combined concern and human tolerance with an obvious awareness of the practical and technical difficulties involved in translating their ideas into a legal form, an awareness almost entirely lacking in the anti-pornography crusade lobby, with their simple-minded enthusiasm for "stamping out" the revolting stuff. Unhappily, many of those who held strong views against pornography and wanted more effective control seemed to have given little or no thought to formulating specific reforms in the law which would deliver the goods, and took some persuading that it was the job of the committee to concern itself not with general lamentations on the state of society, but with legal reform. For example, many criticised the operation of the public good defence, and conceded the need to protect literature and art from repression, but had no idea how these two views could be expressed in legal terms.

Some, for whom the campaigning is I suspect an end in itself, did not particularly care, and said so.

The Emerging Consensus

Until July of 1978 the committee did not hold any prolonged discussion as to what conclusions it might favour; such discussion as did take place was largely informal over coffee or lunch (washed down with some disagreeable vin ordinaire from the Home Office cellars). But certain points upon which a consensus was forming emerged in this informal way. The first was an awareness of the chaotic confusion of the law, which suggested that radical reform was called for; all members were rapidly converted to this, the currently received wisdom. The second involved the acceptance of a theoretical position that the law should only interefere to prevent harm (what the report calls *"the harm condition"*) coupled with the notion that the harm supposed to be brought about by pornography was to be sought in its consequences. Virtually everyone we saw seemed to adopt this position, though disagreeing as to whether harm was in fact caused. The third was an awareness that, whilst the more vocal pressure groups objected to pornography or indeed approved of it for a variety of reasons, general public concern over the matter was largely based not on the fear that it corrupted or depraved people, or caused crimes, marital disharmony or whatever, but simply on the thesis that exposure to it was thought to be offensive or disgusting. "Offensive" is a relatively strong word, and belongs in a spectrum of concepts of which "embarrassing" or "indecent" are at the mild end and "grossly" or "outrageously" offensive, "disgusting", "obscene" (*in the normal not the special legal sense*) at the stronger end. And essentially what is involved here is a breach of accepted social manners of a particular kind which includes a crossing of the line between the private and public.

A Public Nuisance Problem

If it is conceded that the law may legitimately be used to protect individuals from having what is offensive or disgusting to them obtruded upon their attention without their consent, and that being so offended or disgusted counts as a harm, this suggested that at least some forms of pornography should be legislated against, not with a view to eradicating them from society, but with a view to restricting their sale, display, etcetera to avoid offence, or, as lawyers would put it, to avoid public nuisance. There was nothing new in this approach, which had already been expressed, though in an unsatisfactory way, in nineteenth century legislation dealing with indecent displays and advertising, and in the Unsolicited Goods and Services Act 1971. Its logic of course pointed merely to regulating and restricting the outlets for certain forms of pornography so as to avoid offence, and adults who consented to pornography would not require protection. Children would, since they are regarded as not of an age to take certain decisions on their own; I suspect too that we tend to hold a romantic view of the innocence of the young, which we seek to preserve in a world where innocence is not at a premium. We came to call the definition of the material to be restricted as the "outer margin", and the first lengthy discussion of the committee's recommendation was concerned to work out the form restriction should take, and the definition of what should be restricted. The eventual scheme which emerged is set out in essence in the following summary of recommendations:

Restriction

Restrictions should apply to matter (other than the printed word) and to a performance whose unrestricted availability is offensive to reasonable people by reason of the manner in which it portrays, deals with or relates to violence, cruelty or horror, or sexual, faecal or urinary functions or genital organs (paragraphs 9.36 and 11.8).

Restriction is to consist in a ban
(i) on the display, sale, hire, etc. of restricted material other than by way of postal or other delivery and
(ii) on the presentation of any restricted performance other than in premises (or a part of premises having a separate access from the street)
(a) to which persons under the age of eighteen are not admitted, and

(b) to which access is possible only by passing a prominent warning notice in specified terms, and
(c) which make no display visible to persons not passing beyond the warning notice, other than the name of the business and an indication of its nature (paragraphs 9.15 and 11.8).

No material or performance should be exempt from these restrictions on the ground of any intrinsic merit it might possess (paragraph 9.41).

It should be an offence to display, sell, hire etc., any restricted matter or to present a restricted performance in contravention of the restrictions laid down (paragraphs 9.43 and 11.16)"

The breach of the restrictive scheme would be treated on a par with other public nuisance offences, an offence of a relatively minor nature, triable by magistrates and punishable, except in cases of wanton persistence, by a fine.

The policy of merely restricting pornography has obvious advantages, two being of particular importance. So long as the material restricted will, in general, be thought pornographic and the line is not drawn too widely it avoids the need to build into the law elaborate provisions to protect freedom of communication, artistic endeavour, etc. Restricted material will rarely be anything more than porn, and anyway it is still available, just as for example alcohol is. Secondly the scheme is likely to secure the co-operation of those involved in distributing the restricted material, who have little to lose by observing the rules. The committee also went further by excluding the purely written word entirely from restriction, partly because its lack of immediacy deprives it of the power to offend possessed by more visual material, and partly because of its particular importance as a medium for conveying ideas. By 1979, legal action against purely written material under the obscenity laws had, in any event, become more or less impossible, and so this recommendation did little more than regularise the existing state of affairs.

The Problem of the Inner Margin

All this left open three very much more difficult questions. The first concerned what we came to call "the inner margin". Should there be a second category of pornography which should be actually prohibited, which the law should aim to stamp out completely? The second concerned the cinema – should it be treated differently, and subjected either to the existing system of pre-censorship and classification, or to some modified version of such a system? The third concerned live shows, and raised similar questions. It was through its approach to the first and second of these questions that the Williams Report became an object of controversy.

If there was to be an inner margin, a category of pornography to be banned completely, then the basic assumptions which the committee (and most of its evidence) accepted required this to depend upon some harm (other than offensiveness) consequential upon the existence of such material, for merely offensive material was adequately deprived of its ability to harm by segregation and restriction. The point is best illustrated by material blatantly depicting bestiality, which most people would find offensive or disgusting; if the only objection to such material is that, then restriction, not prohibition is called for. Prohibition must depend on some other principle than segregation. In what became perhaps the most controversial part of its report, the committee eventually concluded that in general there was no very satisfactory evidence that pornography caused clearly identifiable consequential harm – much of the discussion turns on the validity of claims that pornography causes sexual offences, since at the time of the report this possibility was much canvassed. It followed that there was no justification for legal prohibitions applying, as some would wish, to some fairly widely defined category of "hard porn", (meaning the most offensive or disgusting material) and in the end the committee settled on the following recommendation:

Prohibition

Prohibited material should consist of photographs and films whose production appears to the court to have involved the exploitation for sexual purposes of any person where either

(a) that person appears from the evidence as a whole to have been at the relevant time under the age of sixteen, or

(b) the material gives reason to believe that actual physical harm was inflicted on that person (paragraph 10.6).

It should be an offence to take any prohibited photograph or film; to distribute or show it, to have it with a view to its being distributed or shown, or to advertise it as being available for distribution or showing (paragraph 10.13).

Prohibited material should be included in the list of goods prohibited from importation, and imports contravening the prohibition should be dealt with according to the normal customs procedures for prohibited imports, save for certain exceptions relating to films (paragraphs 10.13 and 12.48)."

These recommendations confine prohibition to material causing clearly identifiable harm in its production, rather than harm which is consequential upon its distribution. The committee's recommendations as to live shows followed the same basic scheme of thought:

A live performance should be prohibited if

(a) it involves actual sexual activity of a kind which, in the circumstances in which it was given, would be offensive to reasonable people (sexual activity including the act of masturbation and forms of genital, anal or oral connection between humans and animals as well as between humans), or

(b) it involves the sexual exploitation of any person under the age of sixteen (paragraph 11.15)

It should be an offence to present, organise or take part in a performance which contravenes the prohibition (paragraph 11.16).

This scheme of thought was married to the idea that the relative immediacy of the medium involved was important and was also influenced by evidence presented mainly by the Danish police which suggested that live sex shows presented public order problems quite distinct from any generated by the mere sale of magazines in a sex shop. Of course the ballet and drama are to a considerable extent concerned to simulate sexual activity of one kind or another, ranging from bestiality, a recurrent theme in art, down to the romantic contacts of the sitting room comedy; our definition excluded all *simulated* activity from the ban. Otherwise we should have had to build into the scheme some version of the "public good" defence, with all the difficulties that could bring in its train.

The Control of the Cinema

The committee spent a great deal of time studying the workings of the existing system of film censorship, and in viewing and discussing both with the secretary of the Board and other witnesses the problems presented by films, particularly commercially produced films of an extremely violent character; only pictorial violence, particularly on film on video, presents any general problem. It would of course have been simple and at face value consistent with the recommendations which have already been quoted to have subjected the cinema to the same scheme of restriction as applied to magazines and to the same scheme of prohibition. The consequence would of course be the wholesale abolition of pre-censorship and classification by the B.B.F.C., as it then operated. Under such an approach the only *prohibited* films would be those involving child porn and the so-called "snuff" movies, which, some believe, have actually been made. A "snuff" movie is not a movie in which actual death or torture is shown, but one in which persons are killed, tortured or otherwise abused in order to make the film. A solution along these lines would have retained a prior classification system to identify some films as unsuitable for children generally or children of particular ages; such a scheme existed in 1977, for example, in Denmark in spite of the general abolition of any controls there on what adults could see. Classification might also survive for advisory purposes only, but not as a system involving the refusal of certificates to films, for example, depicting bestiality or coprophilia, or some other particularly disgusting or violent activity.

What was recommended instead was the retention of pre-censorship and the power in the censors to refuse certification entirely to films found by the censors to be *"unfit for public exhibition"*. The decision to refuse would lie with the examiners of a new statutory censorship board, and be subject to appeal on the merits to the full Board [The Film Examining Board], but not to the courts. The law would however lay down general principles governing the decision to refuse a certificate, which could be refused:

only if, in the judgement of the examiners, it is unfit for public exhibition. A film unfit for public exhibition should be one that either
(i) contains material prohibited by law; or
(ii) having regard to the importance of allowing the development of artistic expression and of not suppressing truth or reality, is nevertheless unacceptable because of the manner in which it depicts violence or sexual activity or crime (paragraph 12.45)."

Under the same system, the examiners would also classify films

(U) *Suitable for all ages*

(11A) *Children under the age of eleven should be accompanied by a responsible adult*

(16) *No person under the age of sixteen to be admitted*

(18) *No person under the age of eighteen to be admitted*

(18R) *For restricted exhibition only. No person under the age of eighteen to be admitted.*
Certificate refused (paragraphs 12.41–43)."
and **18R** film houses, essentially porno houses but possibly some art houses showing *avant garde* films, would require local authority approval, though in general these authorities would no longer be concerned in film licensing. The law again would lay down principles governing classification:

"In formulating its policy on the control of film content, the Board should be required to have regard to the following guidelines:
(a) the issue of certificates indicating a film's suitability or unsuitability for persons under eighteen should take account of the protection of children and young persons from influences which may be disturbing or harmful to them, or from material whose unrestricted availability to them would be unacceptable to responsible parents.
(b) a film should be classified for restricted exhibition only if its visual content and the manner in which it deals with violence, cruelty or horror, or sexual, faecal or urinary functions or genital organs is such that in the judgement of the examiners it is appropriate that the film should be shown only under restricted conditions."
and **18R** films would only be shown in special conditions. For example:

When exhibiting a restricted film, a designated cinema should be required to make no pictorial display outside the cinema and to display in the foyer a brief synopsis or description of the film prepared by the Film Examining Board (paragraph 12.39).

The Cinema is Different

Obviously, all this depends upon the view that the cinema is in some way different. This view was justified by the committee upon essentially two grounds. One was that film is a more immediate and powerful medium than the printed word or still picture; the second was a policy of caution, based principally on psychiatric evidence, which suggested that extremely violent films might induce violent criminal behaviour:

> *There is certainly no conclusive evidence to the contrary. But there is no conclusive evidence in favour of the belief either . . . it seems entirely sensible to be cautious.*

The type of film which alarmed the committee is illustrated by the film ILSA, HAREM-KEEPER OF THE OLD SHEIKS, one of a series of films belonging to a concentration camp genre; we saw and discussed a number of such films. This includes the threat to insert rats into girls' vaginas, the force-feeding of a girl by tube and the extraction of all of the teeth of one girl in order to facilitate oral sexual intercourse, whipping and torture, the gouging out of an eye, and death caused by an explosive phallus. This film, viewed by the committee, was in my own view by no means as horrific as it might have been, the impact of the film being greatly reduced by its low technical quality: the direction was at a very poor level. Given an abler director and camera crew, much worse was clearly possible. Some films such as the film MANSON (which contains no violent or indecent scenes whatsoever) had been refused certificates by the existing B.B.F.C. on the ground that they might exercise a pernicious effect in society but would not fall within the category of films which the new board would be legally able to ban. Under the scheme the principles of censorship would be legally determined, though the Board would apply them.

The Final Report

In all essentials, the broad scheme of recommendations was settled by the beginning of April 1979 after a meeting at King's College, Cambridge, which was particularly concerned with the inner margin – the material to be prohibited. But there remained much work to be done to work out the scheme in detail and ensure that it could be turned into statutory form, would be workable in practice, and was comprehensive and left no loose ends – one then remaining to be settled was the control of live entertainment. Some of this work was handled by a legal sub-committee and a draft bill was produced within the committee in order to be sure that the recommendations were translatable into legal statutory form, and were workable. As we anticipated, this process threw up certain difficulties and *lacunae.* For example, the definition of the category of prohibited live shows caused great difficulty. But these were ironed out and a draft report, written very largely by the Chairman and Secretary, was ready by the end of the summer. Its comprehensive character was very much the consequence of the work put in during this later period, and in the event it proved acceptable to all members of the committee after quite minor amendments in detail. There was some discussion of the possibility of publishing a draft bill with the report, but its final preparation would have delayed the report, and it had in a sense already served its purpose. In retrospect, it seems to me even more astonishing than it did at the time that the committee not only reached unanimous conclusions – the summary lists fifty-six distinct recommendations – but that throughout the two years of its existence there had never been any real prospect of a radical division of opinion, and very little loss of fur. We parted good friends, having enjoyed our work and apparently each other's company, at about the right time, for none of us had any wish to devote too long a period to the consideration of a subject which, though it has its importance, can hardly be viewed as standing in the forefront of the problems of the world. So having lit the blue paper we, as a committee, retired to a safe distance to await the result.

Chapter 3

The Reception of the Report

Whilst the Williams Committee was at work life in the world of pornography did not of course stand still. In 1977 there were the first stirrings in the long drawn out and, to date, almost wholly ineffective Greater London Council's 'Clean up Soho' campaign; the first feminist demonstration against sex shops there took place in April 1979, and indicated that what was essentially an American movement had reached London in earnest at last. So far as law making is concerned there had also been developments. Back in 1973 the Conservative Government had introduced a Cinematograph and Indecent Displays Bill, based on the report of a Home Office working party on the Vagrancy Acts. This failed to become law because of the dissolution of Parliament in 1974. The Bill was designed to bring all cinema shows either under the licensing system (and therefore effectively under the B.B.F.C.) or under the Obscene Publications Acts, and also had provisions modernising the law on indecent public displays. The Criminal Law Act of 1977 had implemented and modified one aspect of this scheme by bringing *all* cinema shows under the provisions of the Obscene Publications Acts, but had not brought the cinema clubs under the licensing and classification system. Since 1973 a number of attempts had been made by private members to introduce the rest of the scheme. Thus whilst the Williams Committee was sitting the matter was taken up by Mr. Hugh Rossi M.P., but without success, though it was clear that legislation of this character, treating pornography essentially as a public nuisance to be regulated and not as an evil to be extirpated, would have commanded considerable support in Parliament from all sides of the house. Though differing in important matters of detail from the recommendations of the Williams Committee the thinking behind this legislation was very similar to our own.

The Child Porn Agitation

Legislation had however followed upon the nationwide alarm over child pornography in the form of The Protection of Children Act 1978, first introduced by Mr. Cyril Townsend. This alarm began in the summer of 1977, and by the end of June Mrs. Whitehouse was calling for laws to stop the supposed alarming spread of the evil. Certain members of Parliament took the cause up with alacrity, and by November were urging the Home Secretary to act at once on reports that the distribution of child porn was increasing. The Home Secretary, reasonably enough, was reluctant to introduce legislation in advance of the report of the Williams Committee, more particularly because he was unconvinced that there was any special new problem, and was assured by the Director of Public Prosecutions that cases which could not be dealt with under existing legislation hardly ever occurred. Most child porn was in fact imported, and could be seized and destroyed without any legal problems under existing customs legislation as indecent (so long of course as it was detected). But the pressure continued, quite oblivious to rational argument, and on November 24th Mr. Ronald Butt of the TIMES joined the clamour of the more popular press with a clarion call to "Stamp it Out; this abominable evil of using children for pornography" in an article consisting mainly of an intemperate and ill-mannered attack on the then Home Secretary, Mr. Merlyn Rees. He took the opportunity of being rude to the Williams Committee at the same time, doubting whether the members, (about the majority of whom he knew nothing at all), were reliable on the subject:

"Besides, the Williams Committee is quite likely to produce (if the views of some of its membership are anything to go by) a flabby and "progressive" document minimizing the gravity of these problems in false perspectives in the cool "rationality" of committee prose".

In February of the next year he returned to the enjoyable task of ranting on the subject with a piece entitled "Child Pornography: stop the poison now", in which he adopted the extraordinary position of claiming that child porn had not yet started in Britain, a view hardly reconcilable with the known history of this unpleasant subject. The proposal to legislate was welcomed with some reservations in a moderate leader in the same paper the following day. The Home Secretary bowed to an ill-informed clamour, which reached its peak when, a few days later, one Edward Brinicombe drove a lorry up the steps surrounding the statue of Eros at Picadilly Circus and set about it with a chain saw, meaning thereby to make an even more effective protest on the subject. For this bizarre gesture he was subsequently very properly bound over to keep the peace in the sum of £50, and sent the bill for the repairs. Pornography involving still pictures or films of children is, and always has been a particular pornographic genre, and ranges from objectively innocent pictures of nude or scantily dressed children through to material depicting the most extreme and vicious child abuse conceivable.

On the Williams Committee visit to Denmark (as well as in London) I was able to inspect an enormous range of this type of pornography, which was then freely available in the handful of porn shops in Copenhagen, and clearly much of it originated in very poor Third World countries, though some apparently came from northern Europe. Quite a number of the pictures plainly came from very old plates indeed, and only a small proportion depicted extreme cruelty. Material in fact used by paedophiles is widely available in forms not noticed except by the cognoscenti – for example sentimental kitsch paintings of little girls with adult eyes can be bought in High Street shops; presumably it appeals to latent paedophiles. The problem was of course not new in 1977, and the enforcement of the existing perfectly adequate law was impeded by practical and not by legal difficulties; given the massive scale of imports and the container trade it is bound to be very difficult for customs officers to detect such materials unless they have prior intelligence. So, with government support, yet another weapon was added to the arsenal of laws against pornography. The Protection of Children Act covers stills, films, videos, and extends to both the making, distribution and advertising of child porn, but not to its mere possession. It relies on a concept of indecency, and, being largely unnecessary, has in fact been little used, although a number of prosecutions have been brought under it, many of which could as well have been brought under other legislation. Such prosecutions have been used as an argument for the need for a new law, but the argument is quite without foundation.

The Leaking of the Report

Public interest in the whole subject had thus been sustained throughout the two years the Williams Committee had been at work, and Parliament was indeed concerned with Mr. Hugh Rossi's Indecent Displays Bill when the report was in the final stages of preparation. Since the report offered a tougher scheme for the segregation of offensive material than the Bill did the Home Secretary was approached and asked to speed up its publication, which he did, so that members of parliament could have the opportunity of comparison. It was scheduled to appear at 2.30 p.m. on Wednesday, November 28th; the timing of the publication of such reports is curiously related to Prime Minister's question time in the Commons, a report only appearing after the Prime Minister has risen. But before publication day arrived leaks occurred: reasonably well informed versions of its recommendations appeared in a number of papers. For example, the NEWS OF THE WORLD on November 25th put the leaked report on the front page under the headline "It's too Blue for Maggie" next to a showbiz exclusive "Why I still love my randy Scouse git by Mrs. Anthony Booth", and in the GUARDIAN and DAILY EXPRESS on the Monday. A fairly extensive report also appeared in the SUNDAY TIMES, which included the comments of Mrs. Whitehouse: *"It strikes me that we are going from a quicksand into a quagmire, and it is a very very mucky quagmire"* and reference to a group of backbenchers, only one, Mr. Robert Rhodes James, being identified. These leaks were certainly not organised by the committee collectively nor I am sure by its chairman, any other member, or its own secretariat. A careful study of what was revealed suggests strongly that they derived from access to the draft press release, which had of course been prepared in advance of publication, but had not been issued when the leaks appeared. Textual errors suggest that this was read out to journalists but without their having a copy of the text itself. It also appears probable that someone, having obtained the information, hawked it around in order to generate reactions to comment upon. The GUARDIAN'S pre-publication presentation rested upon the fact that a Conservative government was now in power – "Obscenity Report Sets Poser for Government". Norman Luck's piece in the DAILY EXPRESS appeared more sensationally under the heading "Clean up Porn Storm" and opened with the claim that "Tory fury erupted last night over a call to legalise hard porn films and dirty books". It quoted attacks on a report (which they had not of course read) by three Members of Parliament, Robert Taylor, John Stokes and Michael Brown. Mrs. Whitehouse too did not trouble to await publication, believing no doubt that mere ignorance should never stand in the way of the confident expression of opinion; she roundly denounced what she called the 'pornographers' charter'. Mr. Robert Rhodes James was quoted too as being rude when he described the members of the committee as "the last relics of the permissive society", though to be fair to him he made this remark somewhat earlier and in a different context, and had in fact come to love the committee more than these observations would have suggested. By the time the report officially came out from under its wraps there was an air of anti-climax, and it was driven off the front pages no doubt partly for this reason and partly because of reports that a New Zealand DC 10 had crashed in the Antarctic on a sight-seeing flight; the press usually gives precedence to collective death even when the alternative is sex.

The Reactions of the Press

The immediate press reactions were varied. Thus the DAILY TELEGRAPH leader began:

Judged by one simple and valid standard, the Williams Report on Obscenity deserves a welcome: if its provisions were adopted and efficiently applied, they would lead to a dramatic decline in the nation's total consumption of pornograghy.

But the leader writer went on to worry about the "some would say excessively liberal principle" which lay behind the report's emphasis on segregating porn rather than banning it, and went on to express alarm at the proposal to remove all restrictions on the printed word, whilst conceding there were none operating effectively at the time. The writer, who seems to have had young children described to him but may not actually have met any, feared lest "young children" should be free to buy porn at will; no doubt if they did spend their pocket money thus then dental health at least might improve, but I fear the prospects are not good. The TIMES devoted a long leader to the report. This accepted its attitude to the offensiveness of pornography, and the need to segregate it, but criticised the committee for not seeking to use the criminal law to protect adults from the anti-social and criminal actions brought about by its circulation, the implication being that it should be totally banned. The TIMES conceded that *"for rescue from moral and cultural decline a society must turn elsewhere than to the criminal law"*. But in its examination of more tangible harms – crimes and other distinct forms of anti-social conduct – the committee, it argued, had been guilty of inconsistency. For having firmly rejected the evidence offered to it that pornography caused such things it had then, in relation to the cinema, turned a somersault, concluding that films could perhaps cause tangible harm and ought, in consequence, to be subject to pre-censorship. And, on the basis of this purely intuitive judgement *"the committee proceeds without more ado to forge, for the cinema, an apparatus of censorship exceeding in severity anything known at present to the laws of England"*. This change of inconsistency was to be much repeated. The GUARDIAN, somewhat predictably, also favoured the report, as did the DAILY MAIL, which commended *"its commonsense approach"*. Warming to his theme the leader writer just about sustained this purple passage:

The committee has toiled to good effect and has indeed trodden the primrose path between the swamp of permissiveness and quagmire of prohibition on the other.

The DAILY STAR firmly backed the recommendations, as did the LONDON EVENING NEWS:

The Williams Committee on Obscenity has come up with the right answers to some tricky and emotive problems.

Sympathetic too was the SUNDAY TELEGRAPH. Indeed in general the report, though variously received, was given a very favourable reception by the press, though there were doubts and reservations too, as might be expected in so controversial an area. Thus the NEW LAW JOURNAL made much the same criticism as the TIMES had done in relation to the film censorship proposals – this was *"the weakest part of the report"*. The SUNDAY PEOPLE attacked the proposal to introduce the new porno movie category (18R) – *"that would be giving official sanction to filth"*. The SHEFFIELD TELEGRAPH regarded the proposal to tolerate sex shops as somewhat debatable: *"would they not just resurrect and perpetuate the sexual double standards of Victorian England?"*, whilst the BIRMINGHAM EVENING POST attacked, as others did, the proposal to remove all controls from the written word, and the BIRMINGHAM POST raised the perennial problem of defining what precisely was to be segregated under the Williams scheme.

The press also carried news of attacks on the report from predictable individuals, such as Mrs. Whitehouse, though even she, once she had actually discovered what the report said, opinioned that it was not quite as bad as she had initially, in a state of unsullied ignorance, supposed. In the CATHOLIC HERALD Lord Longford made the same concession *("not as bad as I feared")* in an article reflecting his strong personal disapproval of the chairman, against whose appointment he had earlier protested. His principal criticism of the report was that it failed to recommend a much wider area of total prohibition, along the lines of the recommendations of the legal sub-committee of the Longford Committee. This group had recommended not only a policy of segregation by the prohibition of indecent public displays but in addition a total ban on material which outraged contemporary standards of decency or humanity accepted by the public at large and a ban on material produced through human exploitation (a wider category than that adopted by the Williams Committee). Essentially Lord Longford's argument was that the committee (characterised *en passant* for reasons not explained as being confused about children and weak on extra-marital sex) had failed to grasp the true nature of the pornographic evil. He expressed both the hope and the belief "that this report will be a dead duck as far as future legislation is concerned". To date this has proved to be an entirely correct prediction, at least in a formal sense, and it now seems likely that the government's decision to bury the report was taken some considerable time before it reported. From its grave, however, the Report has had some considerable influence, as we shall see.

The Decision to Kill the Report

Such murderous decisions are normally taken at Cabinet committee level, and since these sinister bodies are so shrouded in secrecy that even their membership is not revealed one can only do one's best to deduce what happened from the little available evidence. No doubt this suggestion of a deliberate decision before the Report appeared attributes a high level of deviousness to the politicians and senior civil servants involved, but no one with any experience of them would regard that as a fact which runs contrary to the suggestions I have made. The upper reaches of government are known to be fairly squalid.

Throughout the period when the committee was sitting enquiries were naturally made from time to time as to when the report was likely to appear. On June 28th 1979 Mr. Leon Brittan, who was the Minister of State at the Home Office, replied to a question from Mr. Michael McNair Wilson (which may or may not have been planted) in terms which seemed perfectly innocuous at the time but in retrospect appear very significant. Mr. McNair Wilson, not content with the statement that the report would be available towards the end of the year, pressed on:

May we have an assurance that, as soon as it is in the hands of the Home Office, no great time will elapse before legislation is introduced to make some sense out of the muddle and tangle of the laws which at present cover pornography and indecent displays in order to bring them in tune with a proper sense of morality.

To this the Minister replied in what looks like carefully prepared terms:

The first step necessary after publication of the committee's report is to consider carefully what it says and the reactions of interested people, and thereafter, in the light of that, to consider what legislation, if any, is required to deal with the present position in law.

Both the precise drafting and the timing of this exchange is significant. The committee had met for the thirtieth time on Wednesday 20th June, and did not plan to meet again until 3rd October. For at that meeting the last of its principal recommendations were settled; it merely remained to draft the report and tidy up matters of detail and presentation. I guess Mr. Brittan was aware of this; Ministers can discover what is going on in their departments if they try hard, and there is no reason why they should not. In all probability he would by June 28th have known the broad scheme of the report. His statement now appears to have been a clear indication that the Government, at least if he had his way, was not going to act on the report and proposed to adopt the standard techniques for burying it. Nor need this cause any surprise. The Williams Committee was a legacy of the previous Labour administration, chaired by a person who had long been associated with that party, and it was no part of the style of the new administration to rely on the advice of independent bodies, as the merciless ritual slaughter of many inexpensive and extremely valuable quangos had made clear. Some if not all members of the committee indeed anticipated the Government's attitude, and it was with some prescience, that arrangements were made to ensure the report appeared in a blue cover, (so as to be at least aesthetically appealing to the new administration). A vocal group of conservative members of parliament was violently hostile to any apparent liberalisation of the pornography laws, and all conservative Home Secretaries have to anticipate, and if prudent ward off, the annual savaging from the aggressive right at the party conference. A suspected 'wet', like Mr. Whitelaw, would be hardly likely to go to the wall over a report which, though it might be welcome in some respects, included the proposal to make most pornography freely available to adults, and to remove all controls whatsoever from the printed word, more particularly because his potential enemies within the party were not persons who lost any sleep over the welfare of the arts or literature. As for Mr. Leon Brittan he would no doubt be anxious to establish a reputation for soundness with the Prime Minister, a lady whose inclinations lay more in welcoming the annual assault on her Home Secretary than resisting it. Pornography was not, in any event, a subject upon which the government had any obligation to legislate: the position has been chaotic for years, and the recent clamour over child pornography had been stilled by the passing of the Protection of Children Act. Now it is of course notorious that ministers and senior civil servants deliberately leak information to the press for political ends. Even the provisions of the Budget now appear in advance. It is by no means impossible that the attacks which preceded the publication of the report were aided and abetted, if not organised, *somewhere* within the Home Office, a possibility made more likely by the fact that the journalists of the SUNDAY TIMES, who published the leaks on Sunday November 25, ended their report thus:

It was pointed out in Whitehall that the chance of new legislation as a result of the inquiry was in any case slim before 1981.

It is clear from this that they spoke to an official, who broadly hinted that the Government was going to be in no hurry to act on the report, in line with Mr. Leon Brittan's earlier statement. But although there were obvious political risks in displaying any enthusiasm for the general reform of the law of pornography, there were also risks in doing nothing. Dr. Mawhinney had taken up the Indecent Displays Bill from Mr. Rossi, and there was obviously strong support in the Commons for legislation to curb such displays, which was precisely what the Williams Committee had recommended. If the Commons was permitted to debate the report it might secure such a measure of support from members as to make it difficult not to accept its principal recommendations. So a debate had at all costs to be prevented, Dr Mawhinney and his supporters kept happy, and the opposition to the report be allowed to develop in a way which enabled the government to shelve the matter, at least for the time being. In all this, delay was of the essence.

So it was that Mr. Whitelaw announced in the Commons on the 13th December that he could hold out no promise of a debate: "Such a debate would be very welcome but there are many pressures on Parliament's time". Urged to be bold, he replied that "I had better not be bold now". He explained that "The Government should not proceed without a wide measure of public agreement". Over Mr. Hugh Rossi's Indecent Displays Bill, which he appreciated provided a considerably less stringent scheme of regulation than that recommended by the Williams Committee, he sat resolutely on the fence, indicating that the Home Office would certainly not set out to impede it if the Commons was in favour. A trickle of comments on the report began to arrive at the Home Office; by 10 March some sixty individuals had written in and ten organisations. These predictably included the two most active pressure groups – Mrs. Whitehouse's *alter ego*, the National Viewers and Listeners Association, and the Festival of Light – as well as a number of local government organisations, such as the Association of District Councils and, mysteriously the Bolsover District Council. At this point the Home Office hit upon the idea of starting formal consultations. So letters were sent to a number of organisations (how selected was not revealed) inviting comments on the report. Presumably most of these organisations had already given evidence to the Williams Committee; the technique of posting copies of a committee report to those who have already given evidence to the committee is one of the standard devious practices in this particular trade. The Home Office also announced that it would welcome comments from anyone who cared to write in. All this ensured that the Home Office would receive a substantial body of material from sources bound to be hostile to the report or some aspects of it, and ensured time for the pressure groups to orchestrate protest. Besides, it ensured that the possibility of a Commons debate could be, at least for the moment, postponed. On 31st July Mr. Leon Brittan was able to announce that 1,150 communications had been received, but that the Home Office had still not reached any view on the recommendations; he did not anticipate any legislation being introduced in the current session. The annual conference was not far away, and heaven help a Home Secretary at it if he was known to be in favour of dirty books. I doubt if he would leave the Conference Hall alive.

The Lords Debate

In the House of Lords however there was a debate, initiated by Lord Nugent of Guildford, who had devoted a considerable amount of energy to the subject and had given evidence to the Williams Committee as a member of an all party group of parliamentarians, comprising himself, Lord Longford, Mr. Robert Rhodes James, M.P. and eleven other individuals. The debate took place on the 16th January 1980 and, with a short interruption between 3.49 p.m. and 4.15, lasted from 2.57 p.m. to 9.34 p.m.; some twenty four peers and two Bishops spoke, all fairly briefly, their contributions being limited to ten minutes. The debate reached its low point in the contribution of Lord MacLeod of Fuinary, wherever that is, who produced the immortal remark:

Those of your Lordships who recall the collapse of the Roman Empire will recall the two main factors causing its collapse . . .

The expressions of view were moderately expressed and thoughtful, including those hostile to the report (apart, as one would expect, from that of Lord Longford) and although only a few of those who contributed wholly backed or wholly opposed the report, twelve were broadly favourable, eleven broadly unconvinced, and Lords Barrington, Milverton, Halsbury and Hampton impossible to classify. Lord Belstead, who, as Parliamentary Under Secretary of State for the Home Office, spoke last, naturally sat on the fence, and made a fair comment upon the debate:

I think we have got to face the fact that this debate has shown a fundamental difference of emphasis regarding the balance between prohibition and restriction on the sale of obscene material.

A reservation which quite a number of speakers made was over the recommendation to free the written word wholly from control, though Lord Donaldson pointed out that since the failure of the attempt to prosecute the publisher of INSIDE LINDA LOVELACE back in 1976 this had become the *de facto* position. But this did not allay the anxieties of critics, one of whom, Lord Wigoder, expressed surprise at a recommendation which would mean that THE STORY OF O should be available in paperback to adolescents, unaware apparently that it had been so available for more than ten years.

The Report was of course widely discussed outside

Parliament, and there were numerous radio and televised discussions and commentaries on its proposals, as well as articles in professional and academic journals; the main points of criticism which arose out of all this will be discussed in the next chapter.

The Indecent Displays (Control) Bill

Though time was not found for a Commons debate the proceedings on the Indecent Displays Bill gave the Commons some chance to discuss the subject of pornography and its control. Dr. Mawhinney's attempt to place a version of this measure on the statute book had failed for want of time, though he has enjoyed some measure of government support. Mr. Leon Brittan, muddling his similes, attempted to explain precisely that measure of support as obscurely as possible:

The Government's attitude towards this Bill is rather like that of the fond parent, or perhaps, now that the Bill has been modifed in various ways since we saw the last version, the sympathetic uncle.

It was taken up again by Mr. Timothy Sainsbury and passed its second reading in the Commons on 30 January 1981, eventually becoming law on 27 July of that year. It was the fifth measure of its kind to be introduced since the debate on the Cinematograph and Indecent Displays Bill back in November 1973, all of them unopposed. By January 1981 Mr. Brittan had passed on to higher things, and the Minister of State at the Home Office who handled the matter was Mr. Patrick Mayhew, who, if one reads between the lines, may have been more sympathetic to the Williams Committee than his predecessor. Be that as it may the Government now enthusiastically welcomed the measure. The debate gave Mr. Mayhew a belated opportunity to reveal the results of the contrived consultations and to announce where the Government now stood on the Williams Report

At present I have encountered a wide divergence of views on the Williams Committee recommendations. It is fair to say that the majority of responses to that report that have reached the Home Office have been opposed to them. The Williams Committee considered all aspects of obscenity and indecency in publications and films and it is clear from the report that its recommendations are inter-linked. For example greater restrictions on availability were to be balanced by fewer prohibitions on what could be sold in restricted conditions.

My right honourable friend the Home Secretary made it clear when the report was published that we intended to examine these proposals carefully. We initiated consultations early last year with a wide range of bodies. The greater part of the substantial response we have received has been opposed to the proposals.

The Report in fact lists fifty-six distinct proposals, and without more analysis it is difficult to know what to make of this statement. Be that as it may, Dr. Mawhinney, anxious to see Williams dead and buried for good, asked if the feeling against was substantial enough "to legislate in terms that would be opposite to the Williams Committee Recommendations". What if anything this absurd rhetorical suggestion amounted to it is impossible to say, but the Minister was not to be drawn, merely saying that he could see no early prospect of legislation on the subject. Though in the course of the debate some members expressed regret at the failure to introduce comprehensive reforms the Bill was widely supported both in the Commons and the Lords where the second reading was moved by Lord Nugent:

It will, at least, save us from sex displays flaunting themselves at us from shops and counters, which, of course, it is especially undesirable for young children to see.

Nervous no doubt at identifying himself with the principal policy recommended by the Williams Report, which he had condemned, he thought it prudent to cock a snook at it *en passant:*

The Williams Report which we discussed in your Lordship's house last year is generally thought to be ineffective and unacceptable.

Lord Belstead for the government welcomed the Bill, and the only doubts came from those who were unhappy with its reliance on the concept of "indecency" and those who were repelled (as indeed was Mrs. Whitehouse) by the implication in the legislation of permitting or licensing sex shops which conformed to it. Essentially the Act in its final form follows a policy of segregation similar to that recommended in the Williams Report but much less severe. Indecent matter must not be displayed in public places, or so that it can be seen from them; those under 18 must not be admitted at all to premises purveying such matter, and a specific warning must be displayed so that anyone entering knows the risk. The form was prescribed:

WARNING

Persons passing beyond this notice will find materials which they may consider indecent. No admittance to persons under 18 years of age.

There were numerous exemptions – art galleries and museums, theatres, licensed cinemas and premises belonging to the Crown and to local authorities all fall outside the Act. Whatever else it achieved it certainly simplified the law, for the opportunity was taken to repeal earlier laws on indecent displays, such as s.3 of the Vagrancy Act of 1824. At least it can now be said that most of the law on the subject is in one place.

The Cinematograph (Amendment) Act 1982

It was next the turn of the porno movie clubs and the more recently developed video parlours. It will be recalled that the Criminal Law Act of 1977 imposed the provisions of the Obscene Publications Act on *all* cinema shows, but that clubs giving exhibitions "to which the public are not admitted" were still exempted from the licensing system with the result that they were not regulated indirectly by the B.B.F.C. Under the exemption from the Cinematograph Acts of 1909 and 1952 the porno movie clubs flourished mightily. The change of the law in 1977 made very little practical difference, either because the Obscene Publications Act had become unworkable or because it was not much used against them; if a porno movie house was prosecuted each performance counted as a separate offence, and a determined defence before a jury could paralyse the unfortunate Crown Court concerned for weeks or even months. The Williams Report advocated the closing of the loophole in the licensing system, which also exempted such houses from safety regulations. By 1982 a new spectre had arisen. Under the Cinematograph Act of 1952 a "cinematograph exhibition" is defined as "an exhibition of moving pictures produced on a screen by means which include the projection of light". When the Williams Committee was sitting the received wisdom was that this covered shows produced by the use of video tapes, an opinion which I still think to be correct. By 1982 "The Home Office View" (which I have always thought of as emanating from a creature kennelled deep in the basements of Queen Anne's Gate like some vast phosphorescent queen termite) had moved. Doubts had arisen where a video cassette is shown directly through a television set, the argument being that the picture is produced by electrons striking the interior surface of the tube and not by "the projection of light", though how one can see it if light is not thereby projected escapes me. The Act, another private member's measure sponsored by Mr. Peter Lloyd, brought all cinema shows operated for private gain within the licensing system, and plugged the supposed loophole for some forms of video show. Consequently all porno movie houses are now supposed to abide by precisely the same system of control as the commercial chain cinemas. So too are those more legitimate cinema clubs which are essentially art houses rather than porno houses.

Changes in the System of Film Censorship

The Cinematograph (Amendment) Act is now in force. In September 1982 it was announced that the British Board of Film Censors proposed to introduce a new system of film classification. The old **"U"** certificate would remain, with the explanation "suitable for all" or, with the symbol **"C"** as "particularly suitable for children". But the other categories would change. The old **"A"** certificate would change to **"PG"** – parental guidance, meaning that the Board considered that the film contained material parents might not like their children to see. **"15"** – for fifteen year olds and above; **"18"** – for eighteen year olds and above (the old **"X"** certificate,) and a new category of **"18R"** to cater for the cinema clubs now brought under the censorship system. (**"18R"** films are for restricted distribution only through segregated premises to which no one under the age of 18 is admitted). The change in the name of the **"X"** certificate to **"18"**, and the introduction of the new **"18R"** certificate was recommended by the Williams Committee, after long discussions with the Secretary of the Board, James Ferman. The system includes of course a further non category "Rejected (no certificate)". This is classed "Unacceptable at law", and this probably means that the Board will no longer refuse certificates to "dangerous" films which are not thought to be unlawful (such as the film of the Manson family) though they may only get an 18R certificate. The operations of the British Board are assisted by a body known as the Cinema Consultative Committee, which approved this new scheme, which closely resembles that recommended by the Williams Committee.

The new system is now in operation, and I am told that at the time of writing (late March 1983) some twenty or so films have been classified as **"18R"**; not all of these will necessarily be porno movies. But of course the enormous spread of video has meant that the porno movie house is in all probability a dying phenomenon, and it is significant that the first steps have now been taken by the industry to bring the new world of video under a voluntary system of self-censorship. 'SCREEN INTERNATIONAL' announced in September 1982 that the British Videogram Association had entered into consultations with the B.B.F.C. with a view to classifying video films as films are classified; the Home Office had apparently indicated that unless the video business cleaned itself up there would be legislation imposed upon it. A working party had been established – the members included Dr. Anthony Storr, who was on the Williams Committee – which would investigate the matter and make recommendations. It reported in January 1983 in favour of the adoption by the trade of a voluntary code of practice. This essentially adopts the same system as applies to films – modified in detail to suit the conditions in the trade. Thus videograms will be classified in the same way, **"18R"** videograms will only be sold in segregated conditions, video vending machines selling adult (**"18"** or **"18R"**) videograms will not be accessible to children. A curious feature of the report is its failure to mention who is to do the classifying, and its failure to discuss at all any problems of public accountability in the process. Apparently the task is likely to be undertaken by the B.B.F.C. The operation of the code would be monitored by a Video Standards Council, similar to the Advertising Standards Council. Some minor details of the scheme are still under discussion, but it will undoubtedly be introduced soon. So the B.B.F.C. far from being abolished, as the Williams Committee recommended, seems very much alive and well and living in Soho Square, its future assured at least for the time being, and the video trade is reacting to public criticism in much the same way as the film industry did when the British Board of Film Censors was originally established.

Licensing the Sex Shops

Lurking in the Local Government (Miscellaneous Provisions) Act 1982, alongside provisions dealing with the regulation of ear piercing and acupuncture, and slipped in after the original text of this government measure was introduced into parliament, is a new scheme which may be adopted by local authorities for the control and regulation of sex shops (or as the act grimly calls them "sex establishments"). The Act provides an elaborate licensing scheme which enables local authorities to control both the location and number of sex shops in their area, and explicitly enables an authority which has adopted the scheme to ban them entirely; it also permits control over who can operate such a shop and enables them to be licensed subject to conditions designed to avoid offence and the involvement of minors. The proposals to deal with the public nuisance aspect of porn shops by licensing or planning law techniques was considered and rejected by the Williams Report, so this innovation departs importantly from its recommendations, and it is at the time of writing uncertain what effect this new system will have, in particular how it will apply in Soho, though there is talk of restrictive policy of licensing only a small number of sex shops. "Massage Parlours" – often masturbation parlours – fall outside the system; they could be prosecuted as disorderly houses but hardly ever are, for reasons which may excite the curious. And sex shops are so defined as to include only shops specialising in this trade – no sexual licensing controls apply to shops dealing in other wares but selling a few vibrators or inflatable sex dolls as well.

The Present Status of the Williams Report

The Government has therefore in a sense successfully shelved the Williams Report, and there has never been a Commons debate on its provisions.

It would be surprising if some at least of the members of the Committee were not a little irritated by the somewhat shabby treatment meted out to them, and this point of view was expressed by Polly Toynbee with some feeling in a piece in the GUARDIAN on October 30th 1981 after the Indecent Displays (Control) Act had become law:

Our bone has been buried for us. It looks as if we were useful in keeping the thorny problem of pornography out of the way of politicians for a few years. It's a subject that could hardly be called a vote winner. The Government has not produced a reasoned argument as to why nothing has been or will be done about our recommendations. We do not even know whether the Home Secretary has bothered to read it. Meanwhile this puny, inneffectual and inadequate Bill has been given

Parliamentary time and this week became law, just as if we had never existed.

It is a feeling which I, and I guess other members of the committee, all to some degree share. If however one takes a more detached view it is possible to view the matter rather differently. To the Government the Williams Report did not set a problem because of any fears as to what the country would be like if its recommendations were adopted; indeed the principal burden of its song was to deal with the offence and public nuisance caused by the pornographers, a policy widely supported. Its problematical character lay in its symbolising what may be presented, according to taste, as either rational application of liberal ideology to the problem of pornography or a group of soggy minded progressives too clever by half, going soft on porn and hurrying the country into the mucky quagmire etcetera. No better expression can be found of this than in Mr. Ronald Butt's prediction, set out with a use of inverted commas where his drafting failed adequately to convey his ideological hatred:

"The Williams Committee is quite likely to produce . . . a flabby and "progressive" document minimizing the gravity of these problems in false perspectives in the cool "rationality" of committee prose".

But since 1979 the Home Office and Government have quietly, if largely indirectly, adopted the basic thrust of its recommendations and avoided becoming tainted by an association with the ideology embodied in the report, and the failure to adopt such recommendations as the scrapping of the Obscene Publications Acts, or the freeing of the written text from control, has made little practical difference. In the House of Lords during a discussion of the proposal to license sex shops Lord Bellwin, Parliamentary Under Secretary of State in the Department of the Environment, seems to me to have put his finger on the point when he said of the Williams Report:

"there are wide differences of opinion both in another place and in your Lordships House on the philosophical basis of any such legislation".

But when it comes to practicalities the wide differences rather fade away. For it is clear that to many of those who hold strong views on the subject the issues involved are symbolic, not practical, and for some the battle itself is what matters more than its outcome. It can even become a way of life.

Chapter 4

The Williams Report was of course vigorously criticised, and in this chapter I shall set out the more important criticisms levelled against the recommendations. Most of the objections put forward involved the repetition of arguments which were familiar to the Committee members from their reading and from the evidence which had been submitted, and so the report contains counter-arguments, which I shall not here repeat. It is indeed very difficult to say anything new in this well worn area. However the feminist movement, or rather a modern form of it, has become more articulate on the subject since 1979, and outside the published literature it is now common to hear certain typical feminist arguments advanced in conversation. The Williams Committee did of course consider such arguments (see para. 6.64), but the feminist position is here separately considered in Chapter 5.

Apart from those who would wish to see no laws on the subject whatsoever – not a particularly vocal group – most of the criticisms were directed to showing that the Report had got the boundary between what should be merely restricted on the one hand, and what should be wholly prohibited, or, as the aggressive language of the subject has it, "stamped out", wrong. In addition there were some who, whilst broadly accepting the theme of the Report, raised matters of detail on legal technique. The objections in principle to the Report do not all neatly fall into distinct categories, but I shall set them out under the following heads: objections related to the function of the law, to the appropriate characterisation of pornography, to the use of the so called "harm condition", to supposed internal inconsistency, and, to the special treatment of films and to the special treatment of the written word.

Objections Related to the Function of the Law

The Committee was, as I have earlier emphasised, quite clear in its own mind that it was charged with the job of making recommendations about the law, and in this spirit went to considerable lengths to ensure that its recommendations could be turned into workable legal provisions. Its thinking was throughout profoundly influenced by the view, held by virtually everyone consulted, that the law did not work, a view emphatically restated since the report was published by Lord Denning in **R.** v. **Metropolitan Police Commission ex parte Blackburn No. 2** in a Judgement denigrating both the law and, for good measure, the Williams Committee. Behind all this lies an assumption which is so commonly held as to pass unnoticed – that the primary aim of the law, especially the criminal law, is to influence conduct directly. Thus if, as recently happened, it is made an offence not to wear a seat belt we assume that the object is to influence motorists by threat of penalty to wear them, and if we found that this simply did not happen then the law would seem to have failed. Much of the denigration of the pornography laws makes this assumption – it is claimed that the laws made little or no difference to the availability of pornography, and, so some quite plausibly argue, may actually encourage its production and sale.

But there exists a radically different vision of the thrust of criminal law, according to which it is argued that the primary function is to pass public judgements upon ethical questions and vindicate proper values and standards in society; the law is declaratory and hortatory. Indirectly this may influence conduct, but that is not the immediate aim, and the influence may be seen as involving no more than an arresting of further decline, a keeping of the lid over the steaming pot. Such a view is particularly attractive to gloomy social pessimists, who take the view that things are getting worse, an attitude common to many of those who seek from the law a stand against further decline. *(Some, like Mrs. Whitehouse, actually date the moment when the rot set in, others, like Lord Longford, do not.)* This is the decline and fall theory of Society – we are currently declining, and, if not careful will soon fall. There is still just time to halt the rot.

Some years ago J. M. Finnis, a Catholic academic law yer, set out a theory of the nature of crime which mirrors this declaratory theory of the law's function – crimes, he argued, were not mere sets of forbidden harms. The essence of crime lies in the fact that the criminal "manifests an indifference in some degree to a complex and considerable set of values for which society holds itself responsible". There are a number of leading legal decisions which have expressed this view. Thus in a famous nineteenth century case the Judges refused to accept the idea that in conditions of desperate necessity a man might kill an innocent person to save his own life, even though admitting that individuals placed in a desperate situation might well not heed such a ruling. The value of the decision was seen primarily in its vindication of the sanctity of human life, and in halting a movement which would lead, in the end, to a relapse into barbarism.

Some of the evidence presented to the Williams Committee adopted the declaratory theory, most notably that of the Catholic Social Welfare Committee and the Church of England's Board for Social Responsibility, which argued:

The rationale for the legal control of obscenity as of incitements to racial hatred or (on a broad interpretation) of blasphemy, is the refusal of our society to allow certain basic values – whether of the intrinsic value of human beings, the equality of different ethnic groups, or respect for religious susceptibilities, to be assaulted with impunity.

The Catholic presentation drew attention to the fact that "some people take the law as a guide, in a rough and ready way, for what is right and wrong", and argued essentially that changes to the existing law towards greater liberalisation might be misinterpreted as judgements that pornography was not undesirable – what is often called the "condemn or condone" theory.

Quite a number of critics of the Report tacitly adopted versions of the declaratory theory. In recent times it has been discussed, in my view in a very confusing way, in the context of the disputes centering on Lord Devlin's attack on the Wolfenden Committee Report: a starting point is Lord Devlin's collection THE ENFORCEMENT OF MORALS and Professor H. L. A. Hart's LAW, LIBERTY AND MORALITY. This is discussed in the Williams Report (see paras. 5.3 – 5.14), but the point needs to be made that the celebrated Hart-Devlin controversy, a reenactment of the nineteenth century Mill–Fitzjames–Stephens debate – raises other quite distinct questions, distinct that is from simply a belief in the declaratory features of criminal law. It is concerned also with disagrement as to the proper scope of the criminal law (what sort of conduct should it be concerned with?, what sort of harm should it aim to prevent?) as well as with beliefs about the nature of society, the nature of morality and the notion of morally legitimate authority.

So far as the law governing pornography is concerned the immediate importance of the declaratory theory lies in its implication firstly that the direct effectiveness of the law is not as important as the Williams Committee believed, and secondly that laws against pornography may be legitimate even if more tangible "harms" than damage to values cannot easily be shown to result from its availability.

Objections Related to the Characterisation of Pornography

A number of critics have claimed that the Williams Report failed, as Lord Longford put it in his article in THE CATHOLIC HERALD, "to grasp the true nature of pornography". What seems to be meant by "true nature" here is a characterisation of pornography which embodies a ground for objecting to it. Thus if, as some feminists argue, the true nature of pornography is that of being a form of violence against women, that suggests what our attitude to it ought to be: hostile. Those who have advanced this type of critical argument all reject the notion that the essence of pornography lies in its offensive character (a view, incidentally, which the Williams Report did not espouse, though the Report did regard this as the principal objection to certain forms of pornography). In doing so they do not deny that pornography does offend (Lord Longford himself refers to *"this nauseating subject"*), nor that this calls for action. Their claim is that the essence of pornography does not lie in this feature which of course is shared by other things, such as very dead dogs, which are in no sense pornographic.

What then is the essence of pornography? There are three alternative characterisations offered. One is that it is material which corrupts and depraves – the old legal definition originating in the Hicklin Case got it right. Perhaps another way of looking at the matter would be to say that such critics seek the essence of pornography in the effect it is thought to have on the addict or potential addict; those who attach more importance to its capacity to give offence concentrate their attention on the effect on those who did not like the stuff, and are not in the least addicted to it.

Another view is that the essence lies in fact that the production and distribution of pornographic material entails *exploitation,* and that it is this which is the critical feature. The Longford Committee was particularly concerned with this way of characterising and thereby condemning pornography, and in their draft bill included a special provision penalising those who, for gain, organised its production; many feel that the problem of pornography is essentially a problem about what to do to stamp out pornographers. The analogy here is with the pimp, penalised for *"living on immoral earnings"*, whose legal condemnation was approved by the Wolfenden Committee in a report back in 1957 based on similar principles to those adopted in the Williams Report. The Williams Committee (see in particular paras. 10.6 and 6.68–6.70) recommended the protection of children against exploitation, but broadly left adults to look after themselves; its critics would go further. Arguments cast in terms of *exploitation* tend to divide either into claims that individuals are forced by economic necessity into acting as pornographic models, or into claims that certain "things" (e.g. human dignity) ought not to be allowed to be the object of commerce at all, with or without consent, or into claims that human weaknesses (such as an obsession with bestiality) ought not to be allowed to become an object of simple profit to entrepreneurs. Views of all these kinds were presented to the Williams Committee, and have been advanced since by its critics.

A third type of variant of the characterisation argument essentially belongs to the feminist movement, and is discussed later; it may overlap with the exploitation theory.

Objections to the Use of "The Harm Condition"

The Williams Committee, in common with virtually everyone who gave evidence to it, accepted what it called "the harm condition":

What sorts of conduct may the law properly seek to suppress? An answer to that question which is widely accepted in our society, as in many other societies, is that no conduct should be suppressed by law unless it can be shown to harm someone.

As the report explains this "harm condition", which derives essentially from the philosophical theory of John Stuart Mill, was made the basis of the well known Wolfenden Committee Report of September 1957, whose most controversial recommendation was in general to legalise adult male homosexuality; this became law some ten years later, after controversies similar to those following the Williams Report. The Wolfenden form of the principle is curiously different from and less liberal than the Williams Committee understanding. The function of the law is:

to preserve public order, to protect the citizen from what is offensive or injurious, and to provide safeguards against exploitation and corruption of others, particularly those who are specially vulnerable because they are young, weak in body or mind, inexperienced, or in a state of special physical, official or economic dependence.

Since the Report was published no frontal attack on the harm condition has been launched by its critics, but two less radical points have been taken.

The first raises an empirical question. There has been much discussion as to whether it can be shown by the use of statistics that an increased supply of pornography is positively correlated with an increased volume of criminal offences; arguments have particularly centred upon the crime of rape, and much of the controversy has centred upon the experience of Denmark, where the law was wholly liberalised in two stages in the 1960s so far as adults were concerned, though laws forbidding the sale of obscene material to children and laws restricting the causing of public offence were retained. The principal protagonist of the view that more porn did in some sense lead to more crime came to be Dr. John Court, and the Williams Committee directed a great deal of attention to his work and the controversies surrounding the Danish experience: plainly if he was right then pornography "causes'" very tangible harm. We concluded by rejecting his conclusions, for reasons fully set out in the Report. Dr. Court has, not surprisingly, sought to contest the view the Committee took and written a long critique of the report, not all of it concerned with this particular aspect of the matter. I can only say that this critique (which I have only seen in a typescript version) does not seem to me to carry the argument much if at all further. More generally the enormous amount of scientific or psueudo-scientific literature on the subject continues to grow; a cautious review by E.C. Nelson (PORNOGRAPHY AND SEXUAL AGGRESSION) reaches the conclusion that

"The evidence linking sexually implicit stimuli to harmful sexual and aggressive behaviour is still limited, but none the less suggestive"

but adds, in relation to sex crimes, that the evidence fails to show a link with the viewing of *erotica* generally; he argues that an undifferentiated concept of pornography is not useful. No doubt the literature will continue to increase, but the methodological problems remain.

The second point which has been taken has been made more by implication than in any direct form, and underlies the legislation establishing the scheme for licensing (and potentially banning) sex shops, legislation justified by the claim that they cause environmental pollution. The Williams Report treated the offensiveness of pornography as a harm against which the public could legitimately be protected within the limitations imposed by the "harm condition". The committee then proceeded to analyse the precise nature of this harm, and concluded that it was the offence caused not simply by the external appearance of pornographic material, but by the unrestricted availability of such material. Hence the Report recommended that such pornography should be available only in separate blank window shops, similar to betting shops; however discreetly covered or wrapped it should not be on sale at all in the local newsagents. It considered and recommended against any special planning law controls over shops where it could be sold, or any special licensing arrangements similar to those, for example, which apply to public houses. The scheme proposed in the Report did not necessarily force restricted material into sex shops – that is into shops specialising in the sale of pornography, sex aids and titillating material – though this would often follow. The acceptance of a scheme for the special regulation and licensing of sex shops by the Local Government (Miscellaneous Provisions) Act of 1982 assumes that sex shops can produce bad effects or harms which the Williams Committee's scheme did not obviate; such shops can be regarded as polluting the environment in which they exist, even though they maintain discreet exteriors and exclude the young. Hence a system to control both their number and location.

Objections Related to the Internal Consistency of the Report

The TIMES leader on the Report argued that the Committee, in its treatment of the cinema, was inconsistent with its own priciples, and this criticism has been taken up and commented on by others – notably for example by Enid Wistrich. The argument goes as follows. In Chapters Six and Seven the committee set out their arguments which, it is claimed, show that the case that pornography causes harms (other than offence) is not proven. In para. 5.31 it is argued that the case that harm is caused needs to be proved "beyond reasonable" doubt. The report, with perfect consistency concludes in general that it follows that pornographic material should not be banned, but merely restricted. But when it comes to consider the cinema, conceding that it has not been shown "beyond reasonable doubt" that films cause harm, it nevertheless recommends a new and effective system of pre-censorship which would enable a film to be banned entirely if it was judged by the censors to be *"unfit for public exhibition"* because:

having regard to the importance of allowing the development of artistic expression and not suppressing truth or reality, it is nevertheless unacceptable because of the manner in which it depicts violence or sexual activity or crime.

The conclusion was reached, it is said, because the committee was shocked by seeing some very nasty films, and thereupon rationality went out of the window and emotion took over. Those who want stronger laws argue that this shows the fault in the Committee's principles; the opposing camp berate the Committee for not following out their own logic.

Objections Related to the Special Treatment of the Written Word

The committee recommended that the purely written word should be wholly set free from any censorship or legal control related to its supposed pornographic or obscene character (we were not concerned with other controls, such as libel, official secrets, etc.). I well recall the moment when we agreed to this; one of our members drew attention to the historic nature of the moment when, for the first time in our history, an official body agreed that literature should be free. The proposal attracted considerable criticism – for example from Lord Wigoder, the Bishop of Durham, Lord Tranmire, Lord Longford in the Lords Debate, and by the DAILY TELEGRAPH leader writer. Some critics were particularly concerned that young children might spend their pocket money on purely written pornographic texts; others disliked the recommendation because they though that it would provide a loophole for the development of a new mass pornography industry. Others simply misunderstood the arguments presented in its favour.

Chapter 5

The objections to the Williams Report which have been outlined in Chapter 4 involve no new ideas; all the points raised were considered by the Committee, sometimes at very great length, and, rightly or wrongly, found not persuasive. The radical feminist attack on pornography has however been developed since the report was written, and although the committee did make special efforts to contact modern feminist groups it did not have very great success in obtaining any very clearly set out evidence, directed towards helping the committee in recommending what should be done about the law. There seem to be three reasons and perhaps a fourth for this. The first is that many of the radical groups do not believe in adopting traditional group structures (with regular chairpersons, secretaries and so forth) or in reaching agreed decisions; they prefer to be unstructured and to get along with divergent views. The second is that many radical feminists are not particularly interested in using law to achieve their ends – the law, as they correctly point out, is largely made by men and administered by men. The third is that in Britain radical feminists tend to be associated with the political left, and are not at all happy at any suggestion that they should end up in the same camp as such persons as Mrs. Whitehouse, who belongs somewhere well to the right. The fourth is perhaps that virtually everything which has been produced by the radical feminist movement on the subject is American; there is virtually no independent home product. Any critique of feminist views on pornography is therefore a critique of ideas certainly received in this country, but not originating here.

The Dilemma of the Feminists

The political dilemma to which I have referred is particularly acute in this country, where traditional politics divide into right and left in a way which is not so true of America. It exercises a generally inhibiting effect, particularly on any possible public campaign for stronger laws against pornography, though not so obviously upon other forms of political action of a less orthodox kind, such as marches "To reclaim the night", pickets and demonstrations against shops selling pornography, or the fixing of stickers ("this is offensive to women") on posters which seem to be objectionable. Thus an article in SPARE RIB on the subject in June 1980 entitled "What is Pornography: the opposing feminist viewpoint" offers two types of answer to the question "What can we do?" Ros Coward uneasily suggests "anti-sexist legislation" which would forbid by law "the use of images in language considered degrading to women" but concedes that it might be unenforceable; it would still however have a symbolic function:

a propaganda victory for feminist ideas, rather than letting feminism be swamped with, or by anti-porn, anti-sex moralism.

By this she is referring to the type of legislation called for by such campaigners as Mrs. Whitehouse. WAVAW (Women Against Violence Against Women) a collective offering the opposing view, comes down in favour of picketing:

By organising pickets outside sex shops, cinemas and newsagents we are validating women's anger. And anger is our own response to an industry which exploits, humiliates and degrades us.

Some feminists have however sought to escape from the dilemma, at least at an intellectual level, by setting out a reasoned case for distinguishing the radical feminist objections to pornography from those associated with the political right. The case is argued by Ruth Wallsgrove in an article entitled: "Between the Devil and the True Blue Whitehouse" (SPARE RIB December 1977).

I don't like porn. How then do I differ from Mary Whitehouse? . . . she focusses her attacks on things that are not to my mind pornography at all, but that are worthy, if not entirely successful attempts to educate or explore. She is not solely concerned with images that distort, but also with those that try to describe sex as it actually happens.

This will of course partially solve the problem, but in reality much common ground remains as to what both camps would condemn. The argument moves to stronger ground when it is argued that:

Mrs. Whitehouse's reason for attacking pornography is precisely the opposite to mine. She wishes to maintain the sexual status quo, to preserve the standard roles of women in our society. She is fighting to keep women divided into madonnas and whores . . . She claims to attack porn to protect women, but she does it in the name of the nuclear family and the sanctity of marriage – institutions that oppress women.

Again radical feminists favour sexual liberation, and accuse the Whitehouse camp of opposition to it. But at the end of the day Ms. Wallsgrove predictably rejects legal remedies, preferring that "we . . . should rather stand up together and say what we feel about it", the protest solution. Her ideas are very similar to those expressed in Susan Brownmiller's AGAINST OUR WILL, the Bible of the movement. I am told however that some feminists are now coming round to favour legal action; this for example is the opinion expressed in one of the contributions to the collection TAKE BACK THE NIGHT:

We want to see banned all pornography that portrays rape, torture, murder and bondage for erotic stimulation and pleasure.

But again the function of such a law is conceived of in purely symbolic terms, since it is conceded that the result would merely be to drive the trade underground:

It is better to drive it underground than to see it flourish as an accepted part of our culture.

Radicals however who believe that pornography is essentially a by-product of capitalism place their faith in general political solutions; many do not really address themselves to practical questions at all. The function of their writings is to make the case against pornography, not to provide schemes for realising a utopia from which it would be absent. Thus Andrea Dworkin's PORNOGRAPHY: MEN POSSESSING WOMEN concludes with the claim that:

We will know that we are free when the pornography no longer exists.

and hints that perhaps the tide is turning:

the boys are betting on our compliance, our ignorance, our fear . . . The boys are wrong.

But readers of her book and others will look in vain for the type of legislative proposal associated with more traditional campaigners such as Mrs. Whitehouse, though they too tend to treat such proposals as of peripheral importance. Radical feminists perhaps believe that the function of their writings on the subject is essentially that of raising the consciousness of women, of shaking them out of apathy, not of providing programmes for practical action. Given raised consciousness, other consequences will follow: what they will be they know not, but they will be the terror of the pornographers.

Pornography and Male Domination

There are certain central themes in the feminist literature, and one is that pornography is an expression of male domination and as such one of the mechanisms whereby this is maintained. As such pornography is viewed as expressing an ideology which finds practical expression in the act of rape, an idea embodied in the slogan:
Pornography is the theory: rape the practice.

This supposed connection was one of the themes in Brownmiller's extraordinary and extremely influential book AGAINST OUR WILL. The central thesis of this book, first published here in 1975, is that:

*Rape is nothing more or less than a conscious process of intimidation by which **all men** keep **all women** in a state of subjection.*

The uncomfortable fact that at least in this part of the world very few men ever do rape women is fitted into the theory by this argument:

That some men rape provides a sufficient threat to keep all women in a constant state of intimidation, forever conscious of the knowledge that the biological tool must be held in awe for it may turn to weapon with sudden swiftness borne of harmful intent.

So viewed men who actually commit rape serve as the shock troops in the endless battle to subdue women. Pornography is characterised by Brownmiller as typically presenting women either as victims:

as anonymous, parting playthings, adult toys, dehumanised objects to be used, abused, broken and discarded

or as insatiable nymphomaniacs, and thus expresses what is supposed to be the philosophy of rape. The literature makes not the least attempt to justify this theory, much less to consider other possible alternatives, of which the most plausible would surely link pornography not dramatically with rape but more boringly with solitary masturbation, an activity which is not considered by feminist literature at all.

Pornography and Violence

The other central theme is that pornography may be identified with violence; the slogan claims:

Pornography is violence against women

This in particular is the contention developed in Andrea Dworkin's PORNOGRAPHY: MEN POSSESSING WOMEN, and the suggestion is that the nature of pornography is such that *by definition* it harms women. As the dust jacket of her book succinctly states it:

The question is not: Does pornography ***cause*** *violence against women. Pornography* ***is*** *violence against women, violence which pervades and distorts every aspect of our culture.*

It follows of course from this analysis that attempts to investigate the consequences of pornography (crime rates, anti-social conduct etc.) are wholly misplaced. Indeed pornography is presented not so much as a disagreeable but aberrant social phenomena, a wart on the body politic, but as an integral aspect of the culture. Thus Adrienne Rich's "Afterword" to TAKE BACK THE NIGHT particularly emphasises this point, arguing that pornography is not *"different from the rest of life"* but *"fully in harmony with any culture in which it flourishes"*. Nor is this argument presented against the background of any attempt to analyse pornography into different forms, some catering for more peculiar perversions and some not, some concerned with women, some wholly directed towards homosexual men. Pornography is treated as simply one indivisible phenomenon; it is hard to believe that some feminist writers have ever seen any.

Feminism and Liberal Values

Particular hostility is expressed towards "liberals". Thus Andrea Dworkin's PREFACE specially emphasises this:

Finally, this is not a liberal book about how pornography hurts all of us. As militant feminist Christobel Pankhurst wrote concerning the trade in women in 1913: "Men have a simple remedy for this state of things. They can alter their way of life."

In the writings of Brownmiller there is profund suspicion of liberal values:

". . . a feminist analysis approaches all prior assumptions, including those of the great unquestioned liberal tradition, with a certain open-minded suspicion, for all prior values have worked against the cause of women, and no set of values, including that of tolerant liberals, is above review or challenge".

Where precisely the movement stands on the problem (if there is one) of differentiating between pornography and, for want of a better term, non-pernicious literature, is not easy to see. Brownmiller would clearly not regard LAST EXIT FROM BOOKLYN as pornography, though the male prosecuting authorities did in England; she writes as if what she is talking about – "ugly smut" – is self evident (the elephant fallacy) whilst Andrea Dworkin seems to try to solve the problem by definition:

*The word **pornography** does not mean "writing about sex" or "depictions of the erotic" or "depictions of sexual acts" or " depictions of nude bodies" or "sexual representations" or any such euphemism. It means the graphic depiction of women as vile whores*

and, insofar as I can understand her preface, she reserves her position on any of the questions which might arise over a supposed clash between liberty of expression and condemnation of pornography.

Radical Feminism and the Williams Report

At an immediate practical level radical feminism has nothing to say to so old fashioned an institution as a departmental committee, and the prevailing view within the movement is in any event hostile to the use of the law to stamp out the trade in pornography. At a theoretical level however it is clear that whereas the Williams Committee saw pornography primarily as a public nuisance problem, the harm flowing from it consisting in the offence it caused, many feminists do not accept this. Pornography is seen as a political problem in that it is a mechanism for securing a certain distribution of power in society, one in which women lose out and is in itself an act of violence; the slogan "pornography is violence against women" rejects the notion that the harm produced by pornography is to be sought in the consequences of pornography, but not in the material itself. The claim that pornography degrades women may be seen simply as a way of making the argument for the political significance of pornography as, in the case of some writers, it merely amounts to the contention that pornography is particularly offensive to women, an argument based presumably on the fact that women are more commonly the models in pictorial pornography and the subjects of pornographic literature. The rejection by some radical feminists of any respect for liberal values – such as I suppose freedom of expression – could of course have profound social implications if it was ever to be married to a policy of operating against pornography through the use of criminal law. John Sutherland in his OFFENSIVE LITERATURE: DECENSORSHIP IN BRITAIN 1960–1982 perhaps has this possibility in mind when he concludes his book by quoting a piece from the Guardian (9 December 1981):

Twenty odd years ago the degree of sexual ignorance in this country was so appalling that it was an easy matter for the academic establishment to promote a repressive fascist novelette such as Lady Chatterley's Lover as a beacon of enlightenment . . . Are we still prepared to accept this cheating obscenity?

He comments: *"Griffith-Jones could not have put it more forcibly"*. But this is I feel slightly unfair to that extraordinary creature, who at least made some gestures towards a respect for art and literature:

" . . . let me at once concede that D.H. Lawrence is a well recognised and indeed great writer. Let me at once concede, but perhaps not to so great an extent, that there may be some literary merit in the book".

Radical Feminism and Rationality

Insofar as writers like Susan Brownmiller and Andrea Dworkin may be taken as representative – and these books are certainly the cult books of the movement so far as pornography is concerned, I share a view expressed by John Weightman in a review of Andrea Dworkin's PORNOGRAPHY: MEN POSSESSING WOMEN and the much less extreme PORNOGRAPHY AND SILENCE by Susan Griffin – a man must feel uneasy expressing any view at all about such writings. For, as he points out:

They make no pretence of being objective analyses of the modern phenomenon of commercial pornography. They are rallying calls or war cries intended only for other women.

Effective political propaganda requires simple messages, and the absurd central thesis of Susan Brownmiller's book, that rape is to be understood as *"a conscious process of intimidation by which* ***all*** *men keep* ***all*** *women in a state of fear"*, is the sort of crude thesis which is perhaps the pre-requisite for turning a book which largely consists of rationally presented discussion of the phenomenon into a cult book. Andrea Dworkin's PORNOGRAPHY is a very much more extreme development from AGAINST OUR WILL, and is shot through with bizarre assertions, unlocated in time or space, and presented without the least attempt to justify them rationally. For example:

"Men choose women who are weak as mates (unless heavy is part of the female role) . . ."

"Terror issues forth from the male, illiminates his essential nature and his basic purpose"

"In the United States, the pornography industry is larger than the record and film industries combined"

"Marriage as an institution developed from rape as a practice".

"The poet, the mystic, the prophet, the so-called sensitive man of any stripe will still hear the wind whisper and the trees cry. But to him, women will be mute. He will have learnt to be deaf to the sounds, sighs, whispers, screams of women in order to ally himself with other men in the hope that they will not treat him as a child, as one who belongs with women"

. . . it is more likely that the sexual abuse of boys by close relatives is actually rare because such abuse is potentially dangerous to the adult male . . . the boy will, at some point, be stronger, more virile, than the father".

"In the main, the abominable She is held responsible for everything bad, fearful, or alienating that ever happened to the fully-human He".

With much of what the feminists say about the depressing awfulness of pornography I should not wish to disagree, and certainly pornography is in the main intended for male consumption and presents women in a dehumanised form, though there are of course forms of pornography which do not involve women at all. But lurking behind the savage rhetoric and morbid hatred of men, as collectively responsible for the subjugation of women, which pervades Andrea Dworkin's book, and other similar writings, seems to me at least to lie a fundamental misreading of history. The enormous increase in the availability of pornography in Western societies is a modern phenomenon, but the attitudes to women which the feminists deplore and see expressed and reinforced by it are surely ancient, and in the past the relative position of women in society was very much worse than it is to-day. In a world in which pornography flourishes women are in reality better off, and this suggests to me not of course the perverse view that porn is good for women, but that the size and prosperity of the trade is largely unrelated to the question. Pornography is of course no modern invention, nor are the features of the male character that produce a demand for it. Anyone who has had the experience of life, for example, in a barrack room will know of the relentless obscenity of the conversation of young males. The commercial boom in pornography is to my mind at least a result of the increase in affluence, which, together with certain technological changes, such as have cheapened colour printing, has vastly extended access to material once confined to the rich or relatively rich, and enabled such material, by relying on high quality photography, to become more explicit and consequently more immediately offensive. Whether lewd male fantasy is more or less deplorable expressed in obscene jokes, Rugby football songs or earlier in sea shanties and folk art, or turned into a more passive spectator sport by the Color Climax Corporation or the video tape, it remains a permanent feature of the male character, and fluctuations in the supply of girlie magazines surely make little difference to this fact. In a sense pornography, like convenience foods and plastic litter on the beach is part of the trash of the affluent society, no less and no more significant than other trash, and to view it as the theoretical literature of rape or the subjugation of women is to attribute to it a significance which it lacks. Indeed the general thrust of much feminist writing essentially accepts the fact that porn is no more than an aspect of what John Weightman has called The Abominable-He, and aims to get rid not of porn but of men, at least in the form in which they now exist, an aim which we poor males cannot be expected to support with any great enthusiasm. As the Irish say, God made us.

Chapter 6

Pensées d'Escalier

Several members of the Williams Committee were undoubtedly irritated by the low intellectual quality of some of the attacks made upon it, and by the assumption in the views of some critics that the Committee members had perversely and wantonly failed even to try to consider the evidence presented to them in a dispassionate spirit. Thus David Robinson has written,

A more dispiriting revelation was the widespread inability – shared by people in Fleet Street who should know better – to comprehend that the aim of a Committee of this kind is to analyse impartially the evidence placed before it, and to base any proposals on that analysis. The apparent misconception that a Committee is a group of individuals assembled to pool their personal prejudices exposed this Committee, from the moment it was named by the Home Secretary, to attack from those who felt that their special cause was not specifically represented in its personnel.

Into this camp, presumably because they themselves cannot imagine how Committee members could try to do their job conscientiously, fell such pundits as Lords Longford, Halsbury and Nugent. And bafflement as to how all the members came to agree (more particularly because critics knew nothing of the personal views of the majority of them) led to hints of crafty manipulation by the Chairman. Lord Wigader spoke of "one of the most remarkable feats of chairmanship about which I have ever heard", and Mr. Ronald Butt, (who of all the committee's critics most strikingly illustrated that lack of intellectual dispassion he so readily attributed to the Williams Committee) had recourse to inventing an inner cabinet of evil men:

The Williams Report is built on the unshakable libertarian premise that there is nothing wrong with pornography (who can be surprised in view of the known general views of the ***central*** *core of the Committee?)*

Who belonged to this sinister group, and when and where it met, Mr. Butt did not reveal, nor indeed did he confine his abuse to the central core; all of us were "a handful of Committee sitters using their intellectual agility to verbalise a social problem out of existence". His greatest fury was directed against our view of Dr. Court's evidence:

The pages of the report which dealt with Dr. Court's evidence were, to use the softest word that I can think of, disingenuous and distorted by the worst kind of sophistry

When I rang Mr. Butt and pointed out to him the meaning of the word disingenuous he stoutly denied that he knew what it meant, and on reflection and more extensive study of his writings I imagine he was probably quite sincere in saying this. But irritation passes, and ranters are forgotten, and in the course of time both the argued criticism directed at the report and my own reflection have given rise to some second thoughts: places where one might have put arguments differently, presented conclusions in another way or paused longer.

Consensus and Unanimity

Before outlining such doubts and reservations as I now have a word needs to be said about unanimity – unlike the Wolfenden Committee (which dealt with a similarly tricky subject) the Williams Report was signed by all its members without any reservations; six of the thirteen members of Wolfenden gave only a qualified assent. This unanimity was not achieved by a bullying chairman or sinister inner cabinet; it represented a genuine consensus, without once involving horse-trading. But consensus does not entail totally identical ideas, nor rule out different levels of conviction in the correctness of the result. Thus without much enthusiasm I agreed not to seek to delay the report in order to produce a draft Bill in publishable form; we were all anxious to publish in time for the discussion of the Indecent Displays Bill. In retrospect perhaps we should have delayed, but that is hindsight. Furthermore members probably differed considerably in their vision of what, if anything, would be done about pornography in an ideal world, whilst agreeing upon what form of regulation and control was conceivably acceptable to the public generally in the real world. Unanimity necessarily involves an element of compromise both within the Committee and with the world outside, even if the compromise goes no further than matters of presentation.

The Harm Condition

The committee accepted "the harm condition", as did virtually all of its evidence and witnesses – what if anything should be done about pornography should be determined by an investigation into the consequences of its existence or dissemination. Investigations of this character tend to make use of the concept of causation – does pornography *cause* crime, or the degradation of women, or the arousal of libidinous thoughts, believed, almost incredibly, by some lawyers to be a Bad Thing. Within the framework of thinking dictated by the acceptance of the "harm condition" I have had no second thoughts; thus the treatment in the report of such methodologically misconceived studies as those undertaken by Dr. Court seems to me still correct, and his riposte to the report leaves the matter to me at least where it was. But I am not particularly happy about the "harm condition" as providing a particularly useful tool of analysis when discussing what form the law can take. At one level it generates attempts to apply causal models to diffuse social phenomena involving individual human acts of choice – how can pornography *cause* crime if criminals *choose* to commit them? At another it involves a sort of logical absurdity, for unless one is to pursue a chain of consequences indefinitely there must come a stopping point at which something is bad not because of its consequences, but simply because of what it is. Some toying with a non-consequentialist theory may be found in the Williams Report when values are under discussion – for example in para. 5.24 when it is said that, "The value of free expression does not lie solely in its consequences . . ." and indeed we judge (or 'evaluate') consequences as harmful or beneficial by reference to values, so this must be so. Pre-occupation with the harm condition as a tool in deciding upon the proper scope of the criminal law has long been fashionable, and the fashion was revived by the Hart-Devlin dispute; it may be useful when the concept of harm is narrowly confined to death, physical injury or deprivation of property. But it neglects the value of an alternative analysis which presents the problems in terms of competing values, and recognises that the inculcation of what are thought to be desirable values in society (for example in practical terms the encouragement of good music) is normally not achieved through the criminal law; there is indeed a sort of absurdity in supposing that they could be. We should perhaps have gone into such matters rather more fully than we did, though the problems involved are essentially philosophical. Since the report's publication I have been struck by the number of critics who both assert that pornography is *intrinsically* evil (and imagine that this provides a reason why it should be banned by criminal law) and who go on to allege that it is intrinsically evil *because of its consequences*, as if they could not escape from the language of utilitarianism however hard they try.

The Discrediting of the Law

Before, during and after the Committee sat the chorus of abuse against the law continued; virtually everyone claimed it was unworkable. Reflection seems to me to make this claim suspect at least so far as public display is concerned, and it must be remembered that most complaint had been directed against such display, particularly in the big cities. Under the Criminal Law Act of 1977 the fine for an indecent display went up to £200 maximum (that is for each offence) and there could be imprisonment. Why did we need the Indecent Displays Act? One explanation is that most public displays, though suggestive of appalling scenes within, were not themselves in reality overtly indecent; hence no police action since magistrates would not convict. If so then the complaint against the law was misplaced. Alternatively the police did not try very hard, either because the problem did not seem very serious, generating few complaints, or because of corruption. On the last possibility I suspect that the claim that there are bad laws and bad courts can often form a convenient excuse for bad policing; much of Sir Robert Mark's writings seeks to excuse bad policing in this way. Only give us the tools, the police say, but when they get them life continues as it did before. So in due course new and better tools are demanded by way of excuse.

Principally however criticism was directed against the Obscene Publications Act, and in particular against the operation of "the public good" defence in jury cases. Even here there have been doubts – in Manchester the use of forfeiture proceedings seems to have caused the enthusiastic prosecuting authorities little concern. Where prosecutions are brought under section 2 the court is required to carry out a balancing act between the "obscenity" of the material – in theory its ability to corrupt and deprave – and its artistic or scientific merit, and many critics have found this balancing act, and the elaborate court procedures which it involves, as absurd, and a fundamental weakness in the law. If, as seems likely (for reasons set out in the report, paras. 2.6–2.10) juries have been encouraged to try "obscenity" as a matter of manners there seems to be nothing intellectually absurd in balancing the demands of good manners against claims based on artistic or other merit. What is absurd is for *courts* to engage in this business, and the fault lies not in the form of the law but in the task the law is being called upon to undertake. Nor does it seem to me that the prolongation of trials necessarily means the law is unworkable – it works, but at an unacceptable cost. The Lady Chatterley Trial only took six days, quite a reasonable time to spend reaching a decision on so serious a matter. Blaming the law always suggests that the underlying problems would go away if the law was simplified – for example by getting rid of the "public good defence", as some have argued should be done, (it is suggested that we should no longer be concerned with it.) But the problem would of course remain, for how are we to protect art and literature and science on the one hand and ban books, films etcetera on the other? The merit of abandoning banning in favour of mere restriction is that this dilemma largely disappears; merely abolishing the defence leaves the problem unresolved.

Restriction and Environmental Pollution

The Williams Report largely relied on the restriction of the stronger forms of pornography to the segregated blank fronted shop, adults only being admitted. It discussed, but rejected, regulation by planning control to achieve any of the following objects – limiting the number of porn shops, keeping them away from sensitive areas, such as outside schools, restricting them to red light areas, or scattering them broadly to avoid the development of red light areas. Once the report came out the Soho porn shops, or many of them, soon blanked out their windows and some even put up signs: As Approved By Williams. Children have normally been kept out of them anyway, a policy they have continued. Since then we have had Indecent Displays Legislation, which does not appear to have made much difference. The shop fronts are moderately blank, and the windows contain no dildos or sets of chains and whips; the garish magazine covers can only be glimpsed with some difficulty through open doors or bead screens. But the seedy and rather squalid atmosphere produced by the obvious existence of the sex shops and porno houses remains, and there is somthing particularly repellent about the existence of so many blank shop fronts. The Greater London Council may, under the new legislation, control the number of sex shops and cinemas as well as their appearance, and it will be interesting to see what effect this has. But I suspect that what some have called environmental pollution will continue to exist as a result of the very existence of the outlets of the sex industry. Blank shop fronts and no kiddies does not really grapple with this problem; it goes only some of the way. Hence I now feel that the Report should have gone rather further than it did into the possibilities of dealing with this problem.

There are a number of possible solutions. One is the deliberate creation of red-light areas, which involves not simply zoning the sex shops in but keeping other trades as far as possible out, so as to reduce the need for those who are not sex industry clients to enter such areas at all. A second is to adopt a policy of positively encouraging forms of trading which bypass the problem – typically mail order trading – a policy which could be pursued, for example through tax law. A more radical policy in the long term is to distribute the wares of the sex industry around other trading outlets so that the obtrusive concentration disappears, and the public, one hopes, ceases to be troubled by them. This has happened over the sale of contraceptives, which have come to be accepted on ordinary display in chemist shops, and no longer appear to cause significant embarrassment; once of course they had to be bought in barbers shops. The video boom has had, as one of its consequences, the widespread scattering of soft porn video cassettes amongst the many newly opened shops, which deal in non pornographic tapes as well. Sex shops, ideally, should be encouraged to cease to exist, and it would not be impossible for this policy to be pursued with some imagination. Freeing the written word, as recommended by the Williams Committee, would be a step in this direction; the licensing scheme is a step the other way. It freezes the current structure of the trade, and, by encouraging, through licensing, monopoly conditions, is bound to generate corruption and maximise the profits of the limited number of operators.

The Separate Treatment of the Cinema

That the report is, on this matter, presented in a way which makes it internally inconsistent I could not now deny. The slip lies in para. 5.31 where we argue that legislation against the harms caused by pornography needs to be based on proof "beyond reasonable doubt" that harms occur. Later on in the Report when discussing the cinema we say, correctly, that some of the professional evidence urged caution over a possible connection between media violence and violence in society, and that this, together with a number of other considerations, collectively persuaded the Committee to recommend the continuation of censorship for adults. What we did not say was that there was proof of harm "beyond reasonable doubt" and in this respect alone is the Report internally inconsistent. Nor is it true to say that this decision was based, as the Times leader wrongly implied, simply upon the fact that the Committee "saw a film . . . founds its contents extremely disturbing . . . deemed it unsafe that such a film should be shown". This distorts the argument for effect. In paras. 12.1–12.10 there are seven quite distinct arguments in favour of retaining censorship, and the "nasty films" point (para. 12.8), distorted by the Times leader writer to suggest it was just one film, was presented merely as something which "clinched the argument for some of us". But having put the record straight the question of substance remains – did the Committee merely make a slip in presentation and thus hand ammunition to those who, like the Times leader writer, wanted to discredit the report for other reasons, or did it in fact reach a misguided conclusion?

Certainly I should now present the case differently, not merely dropping the use of the "beyond reasonable doubt" formula, but also arguing the case in terms of what is currently publicly acceptable against a long background of censorship; there is a case for proceeding cautiously and not too fast. I should also, I think, say rather more about the structure of the industry, where near monopoly conditions may not enable the good to compete on fair terms with the bad. But I confess to grave doubts as to whether at the end of the day we should have recommended a system of prior censorship for adults at all. I am now inclined to think that we were wrong. Our recommendations involved substituting for the present hybrid between state censorship and self-censorship a system purely of state censorship, transferring power from the district councils and B.B.F.C. to the new film-examining body. Although a case can be made for the activities of the B.B.F.C. as at present constituted nothing can be argued in favour of control by local elderly bigots, so the ending of the powers of the district authorities would be a gain. But although we built into the scheme for the new Examining Board a number of safeguards – wide composition, a system of appeals, legally defined powers – none of this can offset the dangers of state control over the arts. Recent developments in this country have convinced me of the very real dangers involved, and I am also persuaded by a point made by John Ellis in an article in SCREEN:

> If there is to be censorship of films by the Government body, then this should be a *public* process . . .

It cannot be, since the banning of a film under an efficient system such as we recommended removes the banned film from the public arena. At present this is the position, and our scheme (partially now introduced by the Cinematograph Act of 1981) makes the position worse. Nor is it in any way practicable to removed the defect inherent in censorship. In modern Britain far too much is secret and in the hands of an unaccountable bureaucracy; to establish the new structure would yet again employ the law not to regulate the secret abuse of power but to facilitate it. I am not the only Committee member to have had second thoughts here. The system now being developed to control videograms is objectionable on similar grounds.

The Workability of the Restriction Scheme

All legislation dealing with pornography faces problems of legal definition if it is to operate through the mechanism of the criminal law, and the system of restriction recommended by the Williams Report necessarily faces this difficulty. But for two reasons the problem of definition is not so acute for a purely restrictive scheme of the type we suggested. The first reason is that if the scheme of restriction is likely to secure the cooperation of the trade, as our scheme would have done definition will not attract much controversy. The second is that a definition of material to be segregated does not have to include any exception in favour of art, literature, *etcetera*. Nevertheless the definition we suggested was criticised, as by Lord Nugent in the Lords debate, but since he failed to deal with the full text his arguments are not worth discussing. More significantly. Mr. Geoffrey Robertson thought it too vague, and it is here important to quote the definition in full:

'**8.** Restriction is to consist in a ban
(i) on the display, sale, hire etc. of restricted material other than by way of postal or other delivery and
(ii) on the presentation of any restricted performance other than in premises (*or part of premises having a separate access from the street*)
(a) to which persons under the age of eighteen are not admitted,
and
(b) to which access is possible only by passing a prominent warning notice in specified terms, and
(c) which make no display visible to persons not passing beyond the warning notice, other than the name of the business and an indication of its nature *(paragraphs 9.15 and 11.8).'*

and to set out what restriction would mean:

'**9.** No material or performance should be exempt from these restrictions on the ground of any intrinsic merit it might possess *(paragraph 9.41).*

'**10.** It should be an offence to display, sell, hire etc. any restricted matter or to present a restricted performance in contravention of the restrictions laid down *(paragraphs 9.43 and 11.16).*

'**11.** This offence should not apply to the showing of films, for which we propose separate controls.

'**12.** It should be an offence to send or deliver restricted material, or advertisements for such material, to
(a) a person who the sender knew or ought reasonably to have known was under the age of eignteen, or
(b) a person who the sender knew or ought reasonably to have known had not solicited the material *(paragraphs 9.18–19.)*

'**13.** It should be an offence for a person under the age of eighteen to seek to gain entry to premises in which restricted material is being displayed, sold or hired or in which a restricted performance is being presented, or to order restricted material to be sent to him or her *(paragraph 9.44).*

'**14.** It should not be freely open to any individual to institute proceedings for the criminal offences proposed above; prosecutions should be brought by the police or by or with the consent of the Director of Public Prosecutions *(paragraphs 9.50 and 11.16).*

'15. Restriction offences should be triable only by magistrates and punishable by fines of up to £1,000 and imprisonment of up to six months *(paragraphs 9.43 and 11.16)*.

'16. The police should have power to obtain a magistrates warrant to enter and search premises for material which they believe is being dislayed, sold or hired in contravention of the restrictions, and to seize such material as may be needed for the purpose of evidence *(paragraph 9.45)*.

'17. A magistrates' court convicting an offender for a restriction offence should have power to order, if it thinks fit, that seized material should be forfeited *(paragraph 9.46)*

'18. There should be no separate procedure aimed at the forfeiture of restricted material divorced from criminal proceedings against an alleged offender *(paragraph 9.46)*.'

It will be noticed that this definition and the scheme associated with it is addressed not to the appearance but to the character of the material, and that if offers the public a general definition, leaving to individuals the task of adapting their conduct to the law. Plainly this definition leaves considerable leeway to individual courts, and views as to what falls under it would change over the course of time. There is no escape from this problem unless one adopts one of two other possible techniques. One is to list the rude bits. I see no point in repeating the arguments in the Report which convinced us all of the utter futility of this approach. It sounds plausible until you try it. The other solution, which could work, is to deal with the problem by precensorship through an administrative body, which certifies material as kosher or not. This is Mr. Robertson's preferred solution, and it undoubtedly has attractions. Unhappily unless everything is to be vetted one still requires an offence of selling material which should have been vetted, and one is back to the problem of definition. The Williams Committee rejected this approach for reasons set out in the report (9.22) which I see no point in repeating. But Mr. Robertson needs, I think, to explain how his own scheme (set out in his book at pp. 315–316) would get over our doubts, and indeed his own about vagueness. For example he suggests that the administrative body would have referred to it:

Pictorial matter explicitly depicting specified anatomical details in non-clinical contexts, or photographs of brutal violence.

If this is meant as a definition then (subject to what I will say about the specified anatomical details) it is ludicrously inadequate. He further suggests that there should be an appeal from the Classification

Board to a jury, the jury having to decide both, presumably whether the material fell into the category of material which has to be submitted to the Board in the first place *and* whether it is "manifestly unfit for distribution in the circumstances set out in the original application to the Board". This is all a recipe for a dog's breakfast, and in my view Mr. Robertson has simply not begun to think through the scheme he favours. Those who do favour such an approach would find more mileage in a Board whose imprimatur operates as a defence only; such a scheme is relatively easy to devise but only in conjunction with the first approach.

If at the end of the day the vagueness inherent in all definitions of restricted porn is unacceptable, then that is a case for not attempting to restrict at all.

The Future

In his study of the subject Mr. Geoffrey Robertson has contended that:

The real 'problem of pornography' is the problem of finding any reasonably acceptable alternative to the Obscene Publications Act.

He has in mind in particular the balance which that Act attempted to achieve between two pressure groups – those who knew filth when they saw it and wanted it "stamped out", and those who wanted the law to embody some definite protection for the arts and sciences and for the right of creative artists to explore new territory without having to contend with the excesses of conservative puritanism. I think he is right, and no general reform of the law could possibly proceed without a repeal of the Act. There are those who would approve of such a repeal and of the substitution of a ban, along the lines of existing customs legislation, on the "indecent or obscene", without any form of public good defence. But there is no possibility whatsoever that legislation on these lines could be passed through Parliament. It would of course be possible to achieve the protection of literature under such a scheme by devious means – in particular by retaining official control over prosecutions. Something of this sort exists in relation to the theatre and commercial cinema as it is, and so long as the official (be he D.P.P. or Attorney-General) is not a philistine, the "public good" defence becomes largely otiose. But no repeal of the Obscene Publications Act could be got through Parliament on an assurance of good behaviour by future Directors and Attorneys. So the very existence of the Obscene Publications Act presents an acute problem for any law reformer unless the problem of the public good defence is, somehow or other, bypassed, and here there are essentially only three possibilities. One is to set up a general system of pre-censorship and handle the problem of protecting art and science administratively, as is now done in the case of films. I cannot imagine that any Government is likely to adopt so cumbersome a solution. The second is to abolish all controls, as was done in Denmark; this too is not currently politically possible. The third is to adopt a solution along the lines of that recommended by the Williams Report, which, by concentrating simply on the removal of public offence, bypasses the problem. In effect the Government have largely accepted this solution whilst leaving the pre-existing law, and in particular the Obscene Publications Act, to rot on the vine. This is particularly clearly illustrated over the Williams Report's recommendation to remove all controls from the printed word. To have legislated to this effect would have entailed major amendment to the Obscene Publications Act, with a consequential debate in both Commons and Lords which would have stirred up heaven knows what controversy. In fact for all practical purposes the written word is now free, and one can purchase THE MEMOIRS OF FANNY HILL inexpensively at Victoria Station. By legislation directed at public nuisance coupled with failure to tackle the general reform of the law the Government has as it were contained the problem for the time being. But there remains the risk that the old controversies may be revived by ill judged attempts to use old laws which are in course of becoming obsolete, and the simplest devious technique to guard against this is to enlarge official control over prosecutions. Thus under the Cinematograph (Amendment) Act of 1981 the Director can prevent politically inept private prosecutions of commercial films approved by the B.B.F.C., at least outside the world of the clubs. Broadly speaking Governmental inactivity in relation to the general reform of the law along the lines recommended by the Williams Report can and indeed is going hand in hand with action which produces a practical result not very different. So far as the B.B.F.C. is concerned it has not been formally changed into a government agency, but increasingly close co-operation with Home Office and Director, together with an indirect increase in its powers by the Act of 1981, can go someway along that route, and this is apparently happening. Significantly too the Williams recommendations to introduce the "18R" category once the clubs were brought to heel has been implemented, without public protest. For given the fact that those who call for stronger laws against pornography itself (as contrasted with its public nuisance aspect) are primarily interested in the symbolic force of the law they are unlikely to burst out in protest at anything short of formal liberalisation. What actually goes on does not concern them.

At a purely practical level it is obvious that any policy of "stamping out" commercial pornography could only succeed at enormous expenditure of money, and would require a massive scale of invasion of personal privacy. Cheap travel, the scale of communications, the container trade, the home movie and now the video cassette all make the enterprise quite hopeless. All that can be done is to harass, to beat the pheasants from bush to bush. More particularly modern technology shifts pornography from the public arena into the home; just as we no longer need to go out to the legitimate cinema so we need no longer go out to watch pornography. Porn can, as the advertisers say, be enjoyed in the comfort of our own homes. If a policy of restrictive licensing of trade outlets is vigorously pursued the trade will rapidly either take over the system by corruption or alter its practices by postal or home selling. Harassment will still be possible, and, if the sytem is to work corruptly, so that crime can be farmed, is essential, but in social terms it can have very little effect. It is indeed at least arguable that the bad effects it produces are not insignificant. It would be difficult at any given time to be sure, since the bad effects are necessarily covert.

What could of course exercise a significant effect on the trade in commercial pornography is a change in general public demand or toleration. It is possible that a shift to the approach recommended by the Williams Committee might reduce demand over a long period, though I cannot see how one could be sure of this. So far as toleration is concerned I can personally see no possibility of a reversal of the trend towards greater tolerance of pornography. It is of course simply not the case that in all matters there is now more toleration – a recent re-issue of the Billy Bunter stories had to cut out the original texts of the many flagellant scenes, and public opinion is now much more hostile to racialist literature than was the case in the past. But in straightforward sexual matters toleration has increased, and in a sense this toleration reduces the problem. If nudity no longer offends its social significance is thereby redefined. Thus I doubt whether the campaigners for more rigourous laws are likely to achieve much progress, and the existing laws will, as standards change, appear to them increasingly ineffective. My own admittedly Utopian preference is for a society in which we did not find it necessary to bolster public taste and manners by criminal laws at all, but I appreciate that our society, not yet prepared even for the tale of the Giant Rat of Sumatra, remains unready for so unfearful a state of affairs.

Select Bibliography

Material Published Since the Williams Committee was Appointed

Anon. **(editorial),** *The Times,* 29 Nov. 1979.

R. Butt **'Pornography: does a committee know best?',** *The Times,* 26 June 1980.

J. H. Court, **Pornography and the Harm Condition: A Response to the Report on Obscenity and Film Censorship.** Adelaide 1980

R. Coward, **'Sexual Violence and Sexuality',** *Feminist Review,* 11, 9 (1982).

R. Coward and others, **'What Is Pornography? The opposing feminist viewpoints',** *Spare Rib,* June 1982, p.52.

A. Dworkin, **Pornography: Men Possessing Women.** London, 1981.

J. Ellis, **'Photography/Pornography/Art/Pornography',** *Screen,* 21, 81 (1980).

B. Faust, **Women, Sex and Pornography.** London, 1981.

S. Griffin, **Pornography and Silence.** London, 1981.

L. Lederer (ed.), **Take Back the Night.** New York, 1980.

Longford, Earl of, **'A Porn Report that Fails to See the Evil',** *Catholic Herald,* 14 Dec. 1979.

Nugent, Lord, and others, **Debate in the House of Lords,** 16 January 1980. *Hansard* Vol. 404, col. 115, *et seq.*

C. Pajaczkowska, **'The Heterosexual Presumption. A Contribution in the Debate on Pornography',** *Screen,* 22, 79 (1981).

G. Robertson, **Obscenity. An Account of the Censorship Laws and their Enforcement in England and Wales.** London, 1979.

G. Robertson, E. Wistrich, A.W.B. Simpson, **'Symposium on the Report of the Williams Committee',** *Journal of Media Law and Practice,* 1, 120.

D. Robinson, **'Williams, the Lords and the Press',** *Sight and Sound,* 49, 68 (1980)

J. Sutherland, **Offensive Literature. Decensorship in Britain,** 1960–1982. London, 1982.

M. Tomkinson, **The Pornbrokers,** London, 1982.

P. Toynbee, **'The Williams Committee Worked Hard'.** *The Guardian,* 30 Oct. 1981.

J. Weightman, **'On Her Majesty's (unpaid) Service in the Porn War',** *The Observer,* 12 Dec. 1979.

B. Williams (ed.), **Obscenity and Film Censorship. An Abridgement of the Williams Report.** Cambridge, 1981. *(This contains the full text of the Report, omits the appendices and includes a preface by Bernard Williams.)*

R. Wolheim, **'A Charismatic View of Pornography',** *London Review of Books,* 7 Feb. 1980.

M. Yaffe and E.C. Nelson (eds.) **The Influence of Pornography on Behaviour.** London, 1982.

Appendix A

Reproduced below are the principal provisions of legislation dealing with pornography since the Williams Committee was appointed.

The texts provided are not complete.

Protection of Children Act 1978

An Act to prevent the exploitation of children by making indecent photographs of them; and to penalise the distribution, showing and advertisement of such indecent photographs. [20th July 1978]

Be it enacted by the Queen's most Excellent Majesty, by and with the advice and consent of the Lords Spiritual and Temporal, and Commons, in this present Parliament assembled, and by the authority of the same, as follows:—

Indecent photographs of children.

1.–(1) It is an offence for a person —

(a) to take, or permit to be taken, any indecent photograph of a child (meaning in this Act a person under the age of 16); or *(b)* to distribute or show such indecent photographs; or

(c) to have in his possession such indecent photographs, with view to their being distributed or shown by himself or others; or

(d) to publish or cause to be published any advertisement likely to be understood as conveying that the advertiser distributes or shows such indecent photographs, or intends to do so.

(2) For purposes of this Act a person is to be regarded as distributing an indecent photograph if he parts with possession of it to, or exposes or offers it for acquisition by, another person.

(3) Proceedings for an offence under this Act shall not be instituted except by or with the consent of the Director of Public Prosecutions.

(4) Where a person is charged with an offence under subsection (1) *(b)* or *(c)*, it shall be a defence for him to prove—

(a) that he had a legitimate reason for distributing or showing the photographs or (as the case may be) having them in his possession; or

(b) that he had not himself seen the photographs and did not know, nor had any cause to suspect, them to be indecent.

Entry, search and seizure.

4.–(1) The following applies where a justice of the peace is satisfied by information on oath, laid by or on behalf of the Director of Public Prosecutions or by a constable, that there is reasonable ground for suspecting that, in any premises in the petty sessions area for which he acts, there are indecent photographs of children and that such photographs —

(a) are or have been taken there; or

(b) are or have been shown there, or are kept there with a view to their being distributed or shown.

(2) The justice may issue a warrant under his hand authorising any constable to enter (if need be by force) and search the premises within fourteen days from the date of the warrant, and to seize and remove any articles which he believes (with reasonable cause) to be or include indecent photographs of children taken or shown on the premises, or kept there with a view to their being distributed or shown.
(3) Articles seized under the authority of the warrant, and not returned to the occupier of the premises, shall be brought before a justice of the peace acting for the same petty sessions area as the justice who issued the warrant.
(4) This section and section 5 below apply in relation to any stall or vehicle, as they apply in relation to premises, with the ncessary modifications of references to premises and the substitution of references to use for references to occupation.

Forfeiture.
5.–(1) The justice before whom any articles are brought in pursuance of section 4 above may issue a summons to the occupier of the premises to appear on a day specified in the summons before a magistrates' court for that petty sessions area to show cause why they should not be forfeited.
(2) If the court is satisfied that the articles are in fact indecent photographs of children, taken on the premises or shown there or kept there with a view to their being distributed or shown, the court shall order them to be forfeited; but if the person summoned does not appear, the court shall not make an order unless service of the summons is proved.
(3) In addition to the persons summoned, any other person being the owner of the articles brought before the court, or the persons who made them, or any other person through whose hands they had passed before being seized, shall be entitled to appear before the court on the day specified in the summons to show cause why they should not be forfeited.
(4) Where any of the articles are ordered to be forfeited under subsection (2), any person who appears, or was entitled to appear, to show cause against the making of the order may appeal to the Crown Court.
(5) If as respects any articles brought before it the court does not order forfeiture, the court may if it thinks fit order the person on whose information the warrant for their seizure was issued to pay such costs as the court thinks reasonable to any person who has appeared before it to show cause why the photographs should not be forfeited; and costs ordered to be paid under this sub-section shall be recoverable as a civil debt.
(6) Where indecent photographs of children are seized under section 4 above, and a person is convicted under section 1(1) of offences in respect of those photographs, the court shall order them to be forfeited.
(7) An order made under subsection (2) or (6) above (including an order made on appeal) shall not take effect until the expiration of the ordinary time within which an appeal may be instituted or, where such an appeal is duly instituted, until the appeal is finally decided or abandoned; and for this purpose—

- *(a)* an application for a case to be stated or for leave to appeal shall be treated as the institution of an appeal; and
- *(b)* where a decision on appeal is subject to a further appeal, the appeal is not finally decided until the expiration of the ordinary time within which a further appeal may be instituted or, where a further appeal is duly instituted, until the further appeal if finally decided or abondoned.

Punishments.
6.–(1) Offences under this Act shall be punishable either on conviction on indictment or on summary conviction.
(2) A person convicted on indictment of any offence under this Act shall be liable to imprisonment for a term of not more than three years, or to a fine or to both.
(3) A person convicted summarily of any offence under this Act shall be liable —
(a) to imprisonment for a term not exceeding six months; or
(b) to a fine not exceeding the prescribed sum for the purposes of section 28 of the Criminal Law Act 1977 (punishment on summary conviction of offences triable either way: £1,000 or other sum substituted by order under that Act), or to both.

Interpretation.
7.—(1) The following subsections apply for the imterpretation of this Act.
(2) References to an indecent photograph include an indecent film, a copy of an indecent photograph or film, and an indecent photograph comprised in a film.
(3) Photographs (including those comprised in a film) shall, if they show children and are indecent, be treated for all purposes of this Act as indecent photographs of children.
(4) References to a photograph include the negative as well as the positive version.
(5) "Film" includes any form of video-recording.

Indecent Displays (Control) Act 1981

An Act to make fresh provision with respect to the public display of indecent matter; and for purposes connected therewith. [27th July 1981]

Indecent displays.
1.–(1) If any indecent matter is publicly displayed the person making the display and any person causing or permitting the display to be made shall be guilty of an offence.
(2) Any matter which is displayed in or so as to be visible from any public place shall, for the purposes of this section, be deemed to be publicly displayed.
(3) In subsection (2) above, "public place", in relation to the display of any matter, means any place to which the public have or are permitted to have access (whether on payment or otherwise) while that matter is displayed except—
(a) a place to which the public are permitted to have access only on payment which is or includes payment for that display; or
(b) a shop or any part of a shop to which the public can only gain access by passing beyond an adequate warning notice;
(d) The notice must be so situated that no one could reasonably gain access to the shop or part of the shop in question without being aware of the notice and it must be easily legible by any person gaining such access.

Powers of arrest, seizure and entry.

2.–(1) If a constable has reasonable cause to suspect that a person has committed an offence under this Act he may require him to give his name and address, and if that person refuses or fails to do so or gives a name or address which the constable reasonably suspects to be false, the constable may arrest him without warrant.

This subsection does not extend to Scotland.

(2) A constable may seize any article which he has reasonable grounds for believing to be or to contain indecent matter and to have been used in the commission of an offence under this Act.

(3) In England and Wales, a justice of the peace if satisfied on information on oath that there are reasonable grounds for suspecting that an offence under this Act has been or is being committed on any premises and, in Scotland, a sheriff or justice of the peace on being so satisfied on evidence on oath, may issue a warrant authorising any constable to enter the premises specified in the information or, as the case may be, evidence (if need be by force) within fourteen days from the date of issue of the warrant to seize any article which the constable has reasonable grounds for believing to be or to contain indecent matter and to have been used in the commission of an offence under this Act.

Penalties.

4.–(1) In England and Wales, any person guilty of an offence under this Act shall be liable—

(a) on summary conviction, to a fine not exceeding the statutory maximum; or

(b) on conviction on indictment, to imprisonment for a term not exceeding two years or a fine or both.

(2) In Scotland, any person guilty of an offence under this Act shall be liable—

(a) on summary conviction—

(i) in the district court, to a fine not exceeding £200;

(ii) in the sheriff court, to a fine not exceeding the statutory maximum; or

(b) on conviction on indictment, to imprisonment for a term not exceeding two years or a fine or both.

(3) In this section "statutory maximum", in relation to a fine on summary conviction, means—

(a) in England and Wales, the prescribed sum within the meaning of section 32 of the Magistrates' Courst Act 1980 (at the passing of this Act £1,000); and

(b) in Scotland, the prescribed sum within the meaning of section 289B of the Criminal Procedure (Scotland) Act 1975 (at the passing of this Act £1,000).

Local Government (miscellaneous provisions) Act 1982

PART II

CONTROL OF SEX ESTABLISHMENTS

Control of sex establishments

2.—(1) A local authority may resolve that Schedule 3 to this Act is to apply to their area; and if a local authority do so resolve, that Schedule shall come into force in their area on the day specified in that behalf in the resolution (which must not be before the expiration of the period of one month beginning with the day on which the resolution is passed).

(2) A local authority shall publish notice that they have passed a resolution under this section in two consecutive weeks in a local newspaper circulating in their area.

(3) The first publication shall not be later than 28 days before the day specified in the resolution for the coming into force of Schedule 3 to this Act in the local authority's area.
(4) The notice shall state the general effect of that Schedule.
(5) In this Part of this Act "local authority" means—
(a) the council of a district;
(b) the council of a London borough; and
(c) the Common Council of the City of London.

Section 2 SCHEDULE 3
Control of Sex Establishments
Saving for existing law
1. Nothing in this Schedule—
(a) shall afford a defence to a charge in respect of any offence at common law or under an enactment other than this Schedule; or
(b) shall be taken into account in any way—
(i) at a trial for such an offence; or
(ii) in proceedings for forfeiture under section 3 of the Obscene Publications Act 1959 or section 5 of the Protection of Children Act 1978; or (iii) in proceedings for condemnation under Schedule 3 to the Customs and Excise Management Act 1979 of goods which section 42 of the Customs Consolidation Act 1876 prohibits to be imported or brought into the United Kingdom as being indecent or obscene; or
(c) shall in any way limit the other powers exercisable under any of those Acts.

Meaning of "sex establishment"
2. In this Schedule "sex establishment" means a sex cinema or a sex shop.

Meaning of "sex cinema"
3.—(1) In this Schedule "sex cinema" means any premises, vehicle, vessel or stall used to a significant degree for the exhibition of moving pictures, by whatever means produced, which—
(a) are concerned primarily with the portrayal of, or primarily deal with or relate to, or are intended to stimulate or encourage—
(i) sexual activity; or
(ii) acts of force or restraint which are associated with sexual activity; or
(b) are concerned primarily with the portrayal of, or primarily deal with or relate to, genital organs or urinary or excretory functions.
but does not include a dwelling-house to which the public is not admitted.
(2) No premises shall be treated as a sex cinema by reason only—
(a) if they are licensed under the Cinematograph Act 1909, of their use for a purpose for which a licence under that Act is required; or
(b) of their use for an exempted exhibition as defined in section 5 of the Cinematograph Act 1952 (which relates to exemptions from the requirements of that Act for non-commercial organisations) by an exempted organisation within the meaning of section 5(4) of that Act.

Meaning of "sex shop" and "sex article"
4.—(1) In this Schedule "sex shop" means any premises, vehicle, vessel or stall used for a business which consists to a significant degree of selling, hiring, exchanging, lending, displaying or demonstrating—
(a) sex articles; or

(b) other things intended for use in connection with, or for the purpose of stimulating or encouraging—

(i) sexual activity; or

(ii) acts of force or restraint which are associated with sexual activity.

(2) No premises shall be treated as a sex shop by reason only of their use for the exhibition of moving pictures by whatever means produced.

(3) In this Schedule "sex article" means—

(a) anything made for use in connection with, or for the purpose of stimulating or encouraging—

(i) sexual activity; or

(ii) acts of force or restraint which are associated with sexual activity; and

(b) anything to which sub-paragraph (4) below applies.

(4) This sub-paragraph applies—

(a) to any article containing or embodying matter to be read or looked at or anything intended to be used, either alone or as one of a set, for the reproduction or manufacture of any such article; and

(b) to any recording of vision or sound,

which—

(i) is concerned primarily with the portrayal of, or primarily deals with or relates to, or is intended to stimulate or encourage, sexual activity or acts of force or restraint which are associated with sexual activity; or

(ii) is concerned primarily with the portrayal of, or primarily deals with or relates to, genital organs, or urinary or excretory functions.

Miscellaneous definitions

5.—(1) In this Schedule—

"the appropriate authority" means, in relation to any area for which a resolution has been passed under section 2 above, the local authority who passed it;

"the chief officer of police", in relation to any locality, means the chief officer of police for the police area in which the locality is situated; and

"vessel" includes any ship, boat, raft or other apparatus constructed or adapted for floating on water.

(2) This Schedule applies to hovercraft as it applies to vessels.

Requirement for licences for sex extablishments

6.—(1) Subject to the provisions of this Schedule, no person shall in any area in which this Schedule is in force use any premises, vehicle, vessel or stall as a sex establishment except under and in accordance with the terms of a licence granted under this Schedule by the appropriate authority.

(2) Sub-paragraph (1) above does not apply to the sale, supply or demonstration of articles which—

(a) are manufactured for use primarily for the purposes of birth control; or

*(b)*primarily relate to birth control.

7.—(1) Any person who—

(a) uses any premises, vehicle, vessel or stall as a sex establishment; or

(b) proposes to do so,

may apply to the appropriate authority for them to waive the requirement of a licence.

(2) An application under this paragraph may be made either as part of an application for a licence under this Schedule or without any such application.
(3) An application under this paragraph shall be made in writing and shall contain the particulars specified in paragraph 10(2) to (5) below and such particulars as the appropriate authority may reasonably require in addition.
(4) The appropriate authority may waive the requirement of a licence in any case where they consider that to require a licence would be unreasonable or inappropriate.
(5) A waiver may be for such period as the appropriate authority think fit.
(6) Where the appropriate authority grant an application for a waiver, they shall give the applicant for the waiver notice that they have granted his application.
(7) The appropriate authority may at any time give a person who would require a licence but for a waiver notice that the waiver is to terminate on such date not less than 28 days from the date on which they give the notice as may be specified in the notice.

Grant, renewal and transfer of licences for sex establishments
8. Subject to paragraph 12 (1) below, the appropriate authority may grant to any applicant, and from time to time renew, a licence under this Schedule for the use of any premises, vehicle, vessel or stall specified in it for a sex establishment on such terms and conditions and subject to such restrictions as may be so specified.
9.—(1) Subject to paragraphs 11 and 27 below, any licence under this Schedule shall, unless previously cancelled under paragraph 16 or revoked under paragraph 17(1) below, remain in force for one year or for such shorter period specified in the licence as the appropriate authority may think fit.
(2) Where a licence under this Schedule has been granted to any person, the appropriate authority may, if they think fit, transfer that licence to any other person on the application of that other person.
10.—(1) An application for the grant, renewal or transfer of a licence under this Schedule shall be made in writing to the appropriate authority.
(2) An application made otherwise than by or on behalf of a body corporate or an unincorporated body shall state—

(a) the full name of the applicant;
(b) his permanent address; and
(c) his age.

(3) An application made by a body corporate or an unincorporated body shall state—

(a) the full name of the body;
(b) the address of its registered or principal office; and
(c) the full names and private addresses of the directors or other persons responsible for its management.

(4) An application relating to premises shall state the full address of the premises.
(5) An application relating to a vehicle, vessel or stall shall state where it is to be used as a sex establishment.
(6) Every application shall contain such particulars as the appropriate authority may reasonably require in addition to any particulars required under sub-paragraphs (2) to (5) above.
(7) An applicant for the grant, renewal or transfer of a licence under this Schedule shall give public notice of the application.

(8) Notice shall in all cases be given by publishing an advertisement in a local newspaper circulating in the appropriate authority's area.
(9) The publication shall not be later than 7 days after the date of the application.
(10) Where the application is in respect of premises, notice of it shall in addition be displayed for 21 days beginning with the date of the application on or near the premises and in a place where the notice can conveniently be read by the public.
(11) Every notice under this paragraph which relates to premises shall identify the premises.
(12) Every such notice which relates to a vehicle, vessel or stall shall specify where it is to be used as a sex establishment.
(13) Subject to sub-paragraphs (11) and (12) above, a notice under this paragraph shall be in such form as the appropriate authority may prescribe.
(14) An applicant for the grant, renewal or transfer of a licence under this Schedule shall, not later than 7 days after the date of the application, send a copy of the application to the chief officer of police.
(15) Any person objecting to an application for the grant, renewal or transfer of a licence under this Schedule shall give notice in writing of his objection to the appropriate authority, stating in general terms the grounds of the objection, not later than 28 days after the date of the application.
(16) Where the appropriate authority receive notice of any objection under sub-paragraph (15) above, the authority shall, before considering the application, give notice in writing of the general terms of the objection to the applicant.
(17) The appropriate authority shall not without the consent of the person making the objection reveal his name or address to the applicant.
(18) In considering any application for the grant, renewal or transfer of a licence the appropriate authority shall have regard to any observations submitted to them by the chief officer of police and any objections of which notice has been sent to them under sub-paragraph (15) above.
(19) The appropriate authority shall give an opportunity of appearing before and of being heard by a committee or sub-committee of the authority—

(a) before refusing to grant a licence, to the applicant;
(b) before refusing to renew a licence, to the holder; and
(c) before refusing to transfer a licence, to the holder and the person to whom he desires that it shall be transferred.

(20) Where the appropriate authority refuse to grant, renew or transfer a licence, they shall, if required to do so by the applicant or holder of the licence, give him a statement in writing of the reasons for their decision within 7 days of his requiring them to do so.
11.—(1) Where, before the date of expiry of a licence, an application has been made for its renewal, it shall be deemed to remain in force notwithstanding that the date has passed until the withdrawal of the application or its determination by the appropriate authority.
(2) Where, before the date of expiry of a licence, an application has been made for its transfer, it shall be deemed to remain in force with any necessary modifications until the withdrawal of the application or its determination, notwithstanding that the date has passed or that the person to whom the licence is to be transferred if the application is granted is carrying on the business of the sex establishment.

Refusal of licences

12.—(1) A licence under this Schedule shall not be granted—

(a) to a person under the age of 18; or

(b) to a person who is for the time being disqualified under paragraph 17(3) below; or

(c) to a person, other than a body corporate, who is not resident in the United Kingdom or was not so resident throughout the period of six months immediately preceding the deate when the application was made; or

(d) to a body corporate which is not incorporated in the United Kingdom; or

(e) to a person who has, within a period of 12 months immediately preceding the date when the application was made, been refused the grant or renewal of a licence for the premises, vehicle, vessel or stall in respect of which the application is made, unless the refusal has been reversed on appeal.

(2) Subject to paragraph 27 below, the appropriate authority may refuse—

(a) an application for the grant or renewal of a licence on one or more of the grounds specified in sub-paragraph (3) below;

(b) an application for the transfer of a licence on either or both of the grounds specified in paragraphs *(a)* and *(b)* of that sub-paragraph.

(3) The grounds mentioned in sub-paragraph (2) above are—

(a) that the applicant is unsuitable to hold the licence by reason of having been convicted of an offence or for any other reason;

(b) that if the licence were to be granted, renewed or transferred the business to which it relates would be managed by or carried on for the benefit of a person, other than the applicant, who would be refused the grant, renewal or transfer of such a licence if he made the application himself;

(c) that the number of sex establishments in the relevant locality at the time the application is made is equal to or exceeds the number which the authority consider is appropriate for that locality;

(d) that the grant or renewal of the licence would be inappropriate, having regard—

(i) to the character of the relevant locality; or

(ii) to the use to which any premises in the vicinity are put; or

(iii) to the layout, character or condition of the premises, vehicle, vessel or stall in respect of which the application is made.

(4) Nil may be an appropriate number for the purposes of sub-paragraph (3)*(c)* above.

(5) In this paragraph "the relevant locality" means—

(a) in relation to premises, the locality where they are situated; and

(b) in relation to a vehicle, vessel or stall, any locality where it is desired to use it as a sex establishment.

Power to prescribe standard conditions

13.—(1) Subject to the provisions of this Schedule, the appropriate authority may make regulations prescribing standard conditions applicable to licences for sex establishments, that is to say, terms, conditions and restrictions on or subject to which licences under this Schedule are in general to be granted, renewed or transferred by them.

(2) Regulations under sub-paragraph (1) above may make different provision—

(a) for sex cinemas and sex shops; and

(b) for different kinds of sex cinemas and sex shops.

(3) Without prejudice to the generality of sub-paragraphs (1) and (2) above, regulations under this paragraph may prescribe conditions regulating—

(a) the hours of opening and closing of sex establishments;
(b) displays or advertisements on or in such establishments;
(c) the visibility of the interior of sex establishments to passers-by; and
(d) any change of a sex cinema to a sex shop or a sex shop to a sex cinema.

(4) Where the appropriate authority have made regulations under sub-paragraph (1) above, every such licence granted, renewed or transferred by them shall be presumed to have been so granted, renewed or transferred subject to any standard conditions applicable to it unless thay have been expressly excluded or varied.

(5) Where the appropriate authority have made regulations under sub-paragraph (1) above, they shall, if so requested by any person, supply him with a copy of the regulations on payment of such reasonable fee as the authority may determine.

(6) In any legal proceedings the production of a copy of any regulations made by the appropriate authority under sub-paragraph (1) above purporting to be certified as a true copy by an officer of the authority authorised to give a certificate for the purposes of this paragraph shall be prima facie evidence of such regulations, and no proof shall be required of the handwriting or official position or authority of any person giving such certificate.

Revocation of licences

17.—(1) The appropriate authority may, after giving the holder of a licence under this Schedule an opportunity of appearing before and being heard by them, at any time revoke the licence—

(a) on any ground specified in sub-paragraph (1) of paragraph 12 above; or
(b) on either of the grounds specified in sub-paragraph (3) *(a)* and *(b)* of that paragraph.

(2) Where a licence is revoked, the appropriate authority shall, if required to do so by the person who held it, give him a statement in writing of the reasons for their decision within 7 days of his requiring them to do so.

(3) Where a licence is revoked, its holder shall be disqualified from holding or obtaining a licence in the area of the appropriate authority for a period of 12 months beginning with the date of revocation.

Enforcement

20.—(1) A person who—

(a) knowingly uses, or knowingly causes or permits the use of, any premises, vehicle, vessel or stall contrary to paragraph 6 above; or

(b) being the holder of a licence for a sex establishment, employs in the business of the establishment any person known to him to be disqualified from holding such a licence; or

(c) being the holder of a licence under this Schedule, without reasonable excuse knowling contravenes, or without reasonable excuse knowingly permits the contravention of, a term, condition or restriction specified in the licence; or

(d) being the servant or agent of the holder of a licence under this Schedule, without reasonable excuse knowingly contravenes, or without reasonable excuse knowingly permits the contravention of, a term, condition or restriction specified in the licence, shall be guilty of an offence.

21. Any person who, in connection with an application for the grant, renewal or transfer of a licence under this Schedule, makes a false statement which he knows to be false in any material respect or which he does not believe to be true, shall be guilty of an offence.

22.—(1) A person guilty of an offence under paragraph 20 or 21 above shall be liable on summary conviction to a fine not exceeding £10,000.
(2) A person who, being the holder of a licence under this Schedule, fails without reasonable excuse to comply with paragraph 14(1) above shall be guilty of an offence and liable on summary conviction to a fine not exceeding £200.

Offences relating to persons under 18

23.—(1) A person who, being the holder of a licence for a sex establishment—
(a) without reasonable excuse knowingly permits a person under 18 years of age to enter the establishment; or
(b) employs a person known to him to be under 18 years of age in the business of the establishment, shall be guilty of an offence.
(2) A person guilty of an offence under this paragraph shall be liable on summary conviction to a fine not exceeding £10,000.

Powers of constables and local authority officers

24. If a constable has reasonable cause to suspect that a person has committed an offence under paragraph 20 or 23 above, he may require him to give his name and address, and if that person refuses or fails to do so, or gives a name or address which the constable reasonably suspects to be false, the constable may arrest him without warrant.
25.—(1) A constable may, at any reasonable time, enter and inspect any sex establishment in respect of which a licence under this Schedule is for the time being in force, with a view to seeing—
(i) whether the terms, conditions or restrictions on or subject to which the licence is held are complied with;
(ii) whether any person employed in the business of the establishment is disqualified from holding a licence under this Schedule;
(iii) whether any person under 18 years of age is in the establishment; and
(iv) whether any person under that age is employed in the business of the establishment.
(2) Subject to sub-paragraph (4) below, a constable may enter and inspect a sex establishment if he has reason to suspect that an offence under paragraph 20, 21 or 23 above has been, is being, or is about to be committed in relation to it.
(3) An authorised officer of a local authority may exercise the powers conferred by sub-paragraphs (1) and (2) above in relation to a sex establishment in the local authority's area.
(4) No power conferred by sub-paragraph (2) above may be exercised by a constable or an authorised officer of a local authority unless he has been authorised to exercise it by a warrant granted by a justice of the peace.
(5) Where an authorised officer of a local authority exercises any such power, he shall produce his authority if required to do so by the occupier of the premises or the person in charge of the vehicle, vessel or stall in relation to which the power is exercised.
(6) Any person who without reasonable excuse refuses to permit a constable or an authorised officer of a local authority to exercise any such power shall be guilty of an offence and shall for every such refusal be liable on summary conviction to a fine not exceeding £1,000.

Appeals

27.—(1) Subject to sub-paragraphs (2) and (3) below, any of the following persons, that is to say—

(a) an applicant for the grant renewal or transfer of a licence under this Schedule whose application is refused;

(b) An applicant for the variation of the terms, conditions or restrictions on or subject to which any such licence is held whose application is refused;

(c) a holder of any such licence who is aggrieved by any term, condition or restriction on or subject to which the licence is held; or

(d) a holder of any such licence whose licence is revoked,

may at any time before the expiration of the period of 21 days beginning with the relevant date appeal to the magistrates' court acting for the relevant area.

(2) An applicant whose application for the grant or renewal of a licence is refused, or whose licence is revoked, on any ground specified in paragraph 12(1) above shall not have a right to appeal under this paragraph unless the applicant seeks to show that the ground did not apply to him.

(3) An applicant whose application for the grant or renewal of a licence is refused on either ground specified in paragraph 12(3)(*c*) or (*d*) above thall not have the right to appeal under this paragraph.

(4) In this paragraph—

"the relevant area" means—

(a) in relation to premises, the petty sessions area in which they are situated; and

(b) in relation to a vehicle, vessel or stall, the petty sessions area in which it is used or, as the case may be, desired to be used as a sex establishment; and

"the relevant date" means the date on which the person in question is notified of the refusal of his application, the imposition of the term, condition or restriction by which he is aggrieved or the revocation of his licence, as the case may be.

(5) An appeal against the decision of a magistrates' court under this paragraph may be brought to the Crown Court.

(6) Where an appeal is brought to the Crown Court under sub-paragraph (5) above, the decision of the Crown Court shall be final: and accordingly in section 28(2)(*b*) of the Supreme Court Act 1981 for the words "or the Gaming Act 1968" there shall be substituted the words, "the Gaming Act 1968 or the Local Government (Miscellaneous Provisions) Act 1982".

(7) On an appeal to the magistrates' court or the Crown Court under this paragraph the court may make such order as it thinks fit.

(8) Subject to sub-paragraphs (9) to (12) below, it shall be the duty of the appropriate authority to give effect to an order of the magistrates' court or the Crown Court.

(9) The appropriate authority need not give effect to the order of the magistrates' court until the time for bringing an appeal under sub-paragraph (5) above has expired and, if such an appeal is duly brought, until the determination or abandonment of the appeal.

(10) Where a licence is revoked or an application for the renewal of a licence is refused, the licence shall be deemed to remain in force—

(a) until the time for bringing an appeal under this paragraph has expired and, if such an appeal is duly brought, until the determination or abandonment of the appeal; and

(b) where an appeal relating to the refusal of an application for such a renewal is successful and no further appeal is available, until the licence is renewed by the appropriate authority.

(11) Where—

(a) the holder of a licence makes an application under paragraph 18 above; and

(b) the appropriate authority impose any term, condition or restriction other than one specified in the application,

the licence shall be deemed to be free of it until the time for bringing an appeal under this paragraph has expired.

(12) Where an appeal is brought under this paragraph against the imposition of any such term, condition or restriction, the licence shall be deemed to be free of it until the determination or abandonment of the appeal.

Provisions relating to existing premises

28.—(1) Without prejudice to any other enactment it shall be lawful for any person who—

(a) was using any premises, vehicle, vessel or stall as a sex extablishment immediately before the date of the first publication under subsection (2) of section 2 above of a notice of the passing of a resolution under that section by the local authority for the area: and

(b) had before the appointed day duly applied to the appropriate authority for a licence for the establishment,

to continue to use the premises, vehicle, vessel or stall as a sex establishment until the determination of his application.

(2) In this paragraph and paragraph 29 below "the appointed day", in relation to any area, means the day specified in the resolution passed under section 2 above as the date upon which this Schedule is to come into force in that area.

29.—(1) This paragraph applies to an application for the grant of a licence under this Schedule made before the appointed day.

(2) A local authority shall not consider any application to which this paragraph applies before the appointed day.

(3) A local authority shall not grant any application to which this paragraph applies until they have considered all such applications.

(4) In considering which of several applications to which this paragraph applies should be granted a local authority shall give preference over other applicants to any applicant who satisfies them—

(a) that he is using the premises, vehicle, vessel or stall to which the application relates as a sex establishment; and

(b) that some person was using the premises, vehicle, vessel or stall as a sex establlishment on 22nd December 1981; and

(c) that—

(i) he is that person: or

(ii) he is a successor of that person in the business or activity which was being carried on there on that date.

Commencement of Schedule

30.—(1) So far as it relates to sex cinemas, this Schedule shall come into force on such day as the Secretary of State may by order made by statutory instrument appoint, and accordingly, until the day so appointed, this Schedule shall have effect—

(a) with the omission—

(i) of paragraph 3 above; and

(ii) of paragraph 13(3)*(d)* above;

(b) as if any reference to a sex establishment were a reference only to a sex shop; and

(*c*) as if for paragraphs (*a*) and (*b*) or paragraph 13(2) above there were substituted the words "for different kinds of sex shops".
(2) Subject to sub-paragraph (1) above, this Schedule shall come into force on the day on which this Act is passed.
(3) Where in relation to any area, the day appointed under sub-paragraph (1) above falls after the day specified in a resolution passed under section 2 above as the day upon which this Schedule is to come into force in that area, the day so appointed shall, for the purposes of paragraphs 28 and 29 above, be the appointed day in relation to sex cinemas in the area.

Cinematograph (Amendment) Act 1982

Extension of 1909 Act to certain other exhibitions of moving pictures

1. Subject to the provisions of—

(a) section 7 (application of Act to special premises) of the Cinematograph Act 1909 (in this Act referred to as "the 1909 Act"); and

(b) section 5 (exemption for non-commercial exhibitions) of the Cinematograph Act 1952 (in this Act referred to as "the 1952 Act"),

the 1909 Act and (except so far as they otherwise provide) any regulations made under it shall apply as respects all exhibitions of moving pictures which are produced otherwise than by the simultaneous reception and exhibition of television programmes broadcast by the British Broadcasting Corporation or the Independent Broadcasting Authority or distributed by a system licensed by the Secretary of State under section 89 of the Post Office Act 1969.

Exclusion of exhibitions promoted for private gain from certain exemptions under the 1909 and 1952 Acts

2.—(1) Subject to subsection (2) below, an exhibition which is promoted for private gain shall be excluded—

(*a*) from the exhibitions to which section 7(4) of the 1909 Act (exhibitions in private dwelling houses) applies; and

(*b*) from the exhibitions which are exempted exhibitions for the purposes of section 5 of the 1952 Act.

(2) Subsection (1) above does not apply to an exhibition the sole or main purpose of which is to demonstrate any product, to advertise any goods or services or to provide information, education or instruction.

(3) An exhibition is promoted for private gain if, and only if,—

(*a*) any proceeds of the exhibition, that is to say, any sums paid for admission to the exhibition; or

(*b*) any other sums (whenever paid) which, having regard to all the circumstances, can reasonably be regarded as paid wholly or partly for admission to the exhibition; or

(*c*) where the exhibition is advertised (whether to the public or otherwise), any sums not falling within paragraph (*b*) above which are paid for facilities or services provided for persons admitted to the exhibition,

are applied wholly or partly for purposes of private gain.

(4) If in proceedings for an offence under section 7(1) below any questions arises whether an exhibition was promoted for private gain and it is proved—

(*a*) that any sums were paid for admission to the exhibition or to the premises at which it was given and that the exhibition was advertised to the public; or *(b)* That any sums were paid for facilities or services provided for persons admitted to the exhibition and that the exhibition was advertised (whether to the public or otherwise); or

(c) that the amount of any payment falling to be made in connection with the promotion of the exhibition was determined wholly or partly by reference to the proceeds of the exhibition or any facilities or services provided for persons admitted to it,

the exhibition shall be deemed to have been promoted for private gain unless the contrary is shown.

(5) Where an exhibition is promoted by a society which is established and conducted wholly for purposes other than purposes of any commercial undertaking and sums falling within subsection (3) above are applied for any purpose calculated to benefit the society as a whole, the exhibition shall not be held to be promoted for private gain by reason only that the application of those sums for that purpose results in benefit to any person as an individual.

(6) In subsection (5) above "society" includes any club, institution, organisation or association of persons, by whatever name called.

Applications for grant, renewal or transfer of licence or consent

3.—(1) An applicant for the grant, renewal or transfer of a licence shall give to—

(a) the licensing authority:

(b) the fire authority; and

(c) the chief officer of police,

not less than 28 days' notice of his intention to make the application.

(2) The licensing authority may in such cases as they think fit, after consulting with the fire authority and the chief officer of police, grant an application for the grant, renewal or transfer of a licence notwithstanding the fact that the applicant has failed to give notice in accordance with subsection (1) above.

(3) In considering any application for the grant, renewal or transfer of a licence, the licensing authority shall have regard to any observations submitted to them by the fire authority or by the chief officer of police.

(4) Where, before the date of expiry of a licence, an application has been made for its renewal or transfer, the licence shall be deemed to remain in force or, as the case may require, to have effect with any necessary modifications until the determination of the application by the licensing authority or the withdrawal of the application.

(5) In this Act, unless the contrary intention appears, "licence" means a licence under section 2 of the 1909 Act or a consent under section 4 of the 1952 Act, and references to a licence of either kind shall be construed accordingly.

Appeals against decisions of licensing authority

4.—Any person aggrieved—

(a) by the refusal or revocation of a licence;

(b) by any terms, conditions or restrictions on or subject to which a licence is granted; or

(c) by the refusal of a renewal or transfer of a licence,

may appeal to the Crown Court or, in Scotland, to the sheriff.

(2) Where the decision against which an appeal under this section is brought was given on an application of which (in accordance with section 3(1) above) notice was required to be given to a fire authority and a chief officer of police, any notice of appeal under this section against that decision shall be given to that officer as well as to any other person to whom it is required to be given apart from this subsection.

(3) Where a licence is revoked it shall be deemed to remain in force during the period within which an appeal under this section may be brought and, if such an appeal is brought, until the determination or abandonment of the appeal.
(4) Where an application for the renewal or transfer of a licence is refused, the licence shall be deemed to remain in force or, as the case may require, to have effect with any necessary modifications—

(a) during any period within which an appeal under this section may be brought and, if such an appeal is brought, until the determination or abandonment of the appeal; and
(b) where such an appeal is successful, until the licence is renewed or transferred by the licensing authority.

Powers of arrest and seizure
6.—(1) If a constable has reasonable cause to suspect that a person has committed an offence under this Act he may require him to give his name and address, and if that person refuses or fails to do so or gives a name or address which the constable reasonably suspects to be false, the constable may arrest him without warrant.
This subsection does not extend to Scotland.
(2) A constable or authorised officer of the licensing authority who enters and searches any premises under the authority of a warrant issued under section 5(3) above may seize and remove any apparatus or equipment or other thing whatsoever found on the premises which he has reasonable cause to believe may be liable to be forfeited under section 7(5) below.

Penalties and forfeitures
7.—(1) If—

(a) any premises in respect of which a licence under section 2 of the 1909 Act is not in force are used for an exhibition which requires such a licence;
(b) any premises in respect of which a consent under section 4 of the 1952 Act is not in force are used for an exhibition which requires such a consent;
(c) any premises in respect of which a licence of either kind is in force are used for an exhibition which requires a licence of that kind and are so used otherwise than in accordance with the terms, conditions or restrictions on or subject to which the licence is held;
(d) any premises in respect of which a licence under section 2 of the 1909 Act is in force are used for an exempted exhibition and are so used otherwise than in accordance with the conditions or restrictions on or subject to which the licence is held, so far as relating to the matters specified in section 2(1)*(a)* of the 1952 Act; or
(e) any premises are used for an exhibition to which regulations made under the 1909 Act apply and are so used in contravention of those regulations,

then, subject to subsection (3) below, each of the persons mentioned in subsection (2) below shall be guilty of an offence.
(2) The persons referred to in subsection (1) above are—

(a) any person concerned in the organisation or management of the exhibition;
(b) where a licence of either kind is in force in respect of the premises and the exhibition requires a licence of that kind or as licence under section 2 of the 1909 Act is in force in respect of the premises and the exhibition is an exempted exhibition, the holder of the licence; and

(c) any other person who, knowing or having reasonable cause to suspect that the premises would be used as mentioned in that subsection—

(i) allowed the premises to be so used; or

(ii) let the premises, or otherwise made them available, to any person by whom an offence in connection with that use of the premises has been committed.

(3) It shall be a defence for a person charged with an offence under subsection (1) above to prove that he took all reasonable precautions and exercised all due diligence to avoid the commission of the offence.

(4) A person guilty of an offence under subsection (1) above shall be liable on summary conviction to a fine not exceeding—

(a) in the case of an offence under paragraph *(a)* of that subsection, £10,000;

(b) in any other case, £10,000.

(5) Subject to subsection (6) below, the court by or before which a person is convicted of an offence under subsection (1)*(a)* above may order any thing produced to the court, and shown to the satisfaction of the court to relate to the offence, to be forfeited and dealt with in such manner as the court may order.

(6) The court shall not order any thing to be forfeited under subsection (5) above, where a person claiming to be the owner of or otherwise interested in it applies to be heard by the court, unless an opportunity has been given to him to show cause why the order should not be made.

(7) If the holder of a licence is convicted of an offence under subsection (0) the licensing authority may revoke the licence.

Appendix B

The British Board of Film Censors System of Film Categories.

Reproduced by permission of the British Board of Film Censors.

A MULTI-MEDIA CATEGORY SYSTEM FOR SCREEN ENTERTAINMENT

UNIVERSAL
Suitable for all

PARENTAL GUIDANCE
Some scenes may be unsuitable
for young children

Passed only for persons of
fifteen years and over

Passed only for persons of
eighteen years and over

FOR RESTRICTED DISTRIBUTION ONLY
through segregated premises to which
no one under the age of 18 is admitted

UNIVERSAL
Particularly suitable for children
REJECTED
(no certificate)

Unacceptable at law

BBFC New system of film categories December 1982

At the Cinema Consultative Committee meeting on the 16th September 1982, it was agreed that, in the interests of greater clarity, the following new category system for the cinema will be introduced this autumn:

U – UNIVERSAL. Suitable for all.
PG – PARENTAL GUIDANCE. Some scenes may be unsuitable for young children.
15 – Passed only for persons of 15 years and over.
18 – Passed only for persons of 18 years and over.

There has been general agreement that the **'U'** certificate has proved both useful and generally meaningful to the public. The only clarification here is the new legend, which is intended to be unambiguous in every respect: **'U'** – UNIVERSAL. Suitable for all."

The **'A'** certificate has suffered in recent years from the confusion arising from its being the same symbol as was once used for adult accompaniment, and few parents have seemed to understand the meaning of the warning now implied by it. Films classified **'A'** tend to be unsuitable for young children, and are mostly films designed for more mature audiences which contain some scenes which parents might prefer their younger children not to see. Television surveys have shown that most children prefer to watch grown-up entertainment most of the time, and there are therefore a great many films and television programmes which are made primarily for adults, but from which children need not be barred. On the other hand, many of these films contain some details, possibly of violence or bad language, which are not really suitable for the very young, and parents are generally the best judge of what their pre-teenage children are ready for. The Committee considered whether the **'A'** should be clarified to mean "adult", but this word has unfortunately acquired the wrong sort of associations from its use in phrases like "adult publications" or "adult cinema club", where it is a euphemism for "pornographic". For that reason, it was agreed that the American symbol **'PG'** for Parental Guidance would be preferable, since a change of label would be more likely to lead parents to rethink the meaning of this category and to guide their children accordingly. The current **'A'** category will therefore be altered to: "**PG** – PARENTAL GUIDANCE. Some scenes may be unsuitable for young children." And here the phrase "Parental Guidance" implies both guidance *to* parents about the nature of the film, and guidance *by* parents of their children's viewing.

The **'AA'** category is useful only if it represents films which are truly appropriate for youngsters in their mid-teens, and the crucial factor here is that it should occur at an age which is post-puberty for most children. The current **'AA'** age of 14 has seemed to the Board, as it did to the Williams Committee, to be at least one year too young for this purpose. For that reason, the Cinema Consultative Committee has agreed to raise the age from 14 to 15. The letters **'AA'**, introduced in 1970, have proved meaningless or misleading to many people, being taken to mean "adult accompaniment" by too many parents. Thus, the use of these letters will be phased out and a simple numerical age category substituted as is done throughout the rest of Europe.

The **'X'** category has proved its usefulness as referring to adult films suitable for showing in the public cinema. Unfortunately, in recent years, the letter **'X'** has become widely associated with sex content, despite the fact that fewer and fewer sex films are included in this category. Indeed, Britain is the only country in the world which now uses **'X'** as a category label for respectable adult films. In America and France, the **'X'** is used only for hardcore pornography, and Australia has recently suggested the introduction of an **'X'** for the same purpose. For that reason, a numerical label **'18'**, will be introduced for this category, as for the **'AA'**.

The change to numerical symbols for the **'AA'** and **'X'** certificates may take some time to become familiar, and the film industry has asked that, for two years, the old categories should be listed in brackets after **'15'** and **'18'** for purposes of advertising and front-of-house information. The form used will be the following:

15 (AA) – Passed only for persons of 15 years and over.
18 (X) – Passed only for persons of 18 years and over.

The clarity of all the above categories will, we hope, enable them to be used for video, cable or satellite TV as well, since they will for the most part be self-explanatory.

The Committee also approved, in principle, the introduction of a new **'Restricted 18'** category for films to be exhibited only in specifically licensed premises to which no one under the age of 18 would be admitted. These will normally be either club cinemas or exhibition areas of sex shops licensed under the new Local Government (Miscellaneous Provisions) Act. This extra category will carry the following explanation:

Restricted 18 – For restricted distribution only, through specifically licensed premises to which no one under the age of 18 is admitted.

The licensing conditions which must be observed by cinemas exhibiting films in this restricted category are currently being drafted by the Home Office.

The target date for introducing the new category system will be 19th December 1982.

The Cinema Consultative Committee includes representatives of the local licensing authorities and the film industry trade associations. It meets from time to time to discuss changes in the licensing arrangements for cinema exhibition in Britain. The President of the British Board of Film Censors takes the Chair, and representatives of the Home Office and the Scottish Home and Health Department attend as observers.

James Ferman Secretary British Board of Film Censors

Appendix C

The Report of the Video Working Party

Reproduced by permission of the British Videogram Association Ltd.

Report of The Video Working Party convened by the British Board of Film Censors at the request of the British Videogram Association

January 1983

Preface

by the two members of the Working Party who represent the sponsors, The British Videogram Association

We are grateful for the time and care and the understanding which our distinguished colleagues have given to this task. We record our gratitude also to Lord Harlech, President of the British Board of Film Censors, to the dedicated staff of the Board, and particularly to James Ferman, Secretary of the BBFC, whose commitment illuminates every section of this document.

We welcome the proposed categories, are happy that the cinema industry has adopted them and are pleased that our particular request has been met for some means of making a positive recommendation of videograms suitable for children.

This was the essence of the BVA's commission to the BBFC. We have felt that a simple system of product labelling could be helpful – enabling each consumer to make his or her own decision whether or not to view a particular videogram, and we believe that the symbol and the précis will meet this need. We have argued strongly that any burden of justification should fall on those who wish to introduce restrictions – it is not for the consumer to defend his new freedom of choice.

The BVA led the offensive against video "nasties" as whole-heartedly as the attack on copyright theft – our 70 member companies have amply demonstrated their determination to build a responsible as well as a popular new industry. We commend this report to them, to wholesalers and retailers of videograms, and to everyone who cares.

Donald MacLean
Chairman
British Video Association

Norman Abbott
Chief Executive
British Video Association

A Request from the Industry

(1) The British Videogram Association, on behalf of publishers and distributors of video cassettes and video discs, has asked the British Board of Film Censors to set up a Working Party to consider the means by which pre-recorded video might become subject to the same system of certification which has operated in Britain for theatrical films. Experts in the fields of broadcasting, psychology and the law were invited to serve on the Working Party and to offer guidance on the degree of protection needed for children as well as the kinds of advice which should be given to parents both as customers and as owners of a video recorder. The

Working Party also had regard to the knowledge which video publishers and dealers must have in order to fulfill legal and social responsibilities.

(2) In pursuing these matters, members of the Working Party examined in some detail the system of cinema categories operating in Britain since 1970 and considered ways in which these categories might be improved so as to make them applicable not only to home video but to the new technologies of cable and satellite television. With moving pictures being delivered through so many different media of screen communications, it seemed desirable that the classifications in use for home video should aim at parity with those applicable to the other technologies, the categories being universal but their implications being specific to each medium. And since the usefulness of any such system depends on a reasonable degree of compliance from all concerned, the Working Party had to consider how these categories might be administered through a regulatory process which would demonstrate the willingness of this rapidly growing industry to serve the interests of both its customers and the public at large.

(3) The importance of video in British society, and the speed with which it has established itself in less than three years, may be measured by two statistics: by 1982, one in ten British households was equipped with a video recorder, and there were more video shops in Britain than bookshops. Whatever the success of cable and satellite TV, the spread of video recording and playback equipment is likely to continue, and the sale or hire of pre-recorded cassettes to be played on this equipment will continue as well. Movies on video for viewing in the home will soon be within the grasp of most families in Britain, and there are problems to be faced as well as opportunities.

The Nature of the Problem

Consumer safeguards

(4) In requesting this study, the British Videogram Association hoped first of all to introduce a system of safeguards to protect members of the public from inadvertently buying or renting videograms which might be grossly offensive to some adults or seriously disturbing children. The release on video during 1982 of films which would probably have been banned from the cinema circuits has made it essential that the public should be fully aware of the contents of any videograms they might acquire. And a system of classification similar to that operating in the cinema is a first step in this process.

The law

(5) It was anticipated by the BVA that some of the material submitted for classification could be found so offensive or potentially harmful that it would fall outside the category system adopted for the industry. Some videograms on release in Britain have already been judged obscene by the courts, and it has been recognised by the Association that the legality of all material published by their member companies is essential. There was no wish to interfere with the right of every producer to publish material which is within the law, but the requirements of the law, and particularly those provisions protecting the health and welfare of children and young persons, must be observed.

(6) In approaching the British Board of Film Censors, the BVA was aware that the Board has always applied the appropriate legal tests before granting a film a certificate for the licensed cinema. Indeed, this duty was laid on all local authorities by the Court of Appeal in 1976, and the BBFC, which exercises a delegated function on behalf of statutory licensing

authorities, has assumed this responsibility ever since. No film is passed for the cinema which is judged to be in breach of any test of British law, and a similar legal pre-vetting of videograms has been seen by the BVA as an integral part of the certification process.

Ground rules for the media

(7) The criminal law sets limits to what is broadly permissible in the field of publication, but within those limits there have been traditional requirements laid down in cinema licences and in the regulations governing broadcasting prohibiting "matter which, if exhibited, would offend against good taste or decency or would be likely to encourage or incite to crime or to lead to disorder or to be offensive to public feeling." The Hunt Committee, in its Report on Cable Expansion and Broadcasting Policy, considered whether these ground rules should apply to cable as well and concluded that, for the most part, they should. Their reasoning is worth quoting:

"We have carefully considered the thesis that a cable television system, as a result of its diversity, can be seen as just another branch of publishing, subject only to the laws on such matters as defamation, sedition, and obscenity. We believe this approach might become acceptable when the whole country is cabled, if there is then genuinely the same sort of choice as is found in a bookshop, and if there is a general consensus about what has, and what has not, got a place on cable television . . . [but] the weight of evidence submitted to us strongly suggests that most people still see the carrying of programmes into the home as different in kind from the act of going out to buy a book or a magazine. A book is read alone, whereas much television is watched by the family as a whole. Furthermore, we agree with the Williams Committee that film with all its associated techniques of close-up and special effects is a uniquely powerful instrument, and we regard video material as within the same category."

(Hunt, Cmnd 8679, page 4, paragraph 11).

Private and deliberate choice

(8) Although Hunt brackets video with cable here, the position of pre-recorded videograms is rather different in some respects. Of all the media of screen entertainment, video is the one which permits the greatest degree of private and deliberate choice. A videogram is a physical entity, obtained from a shop much like a bookshop and selected from a wide choice of available material. It is carried home privately by the consumer, to be viewed in private whenever and in whatever circumstances he chooses. There is no common carrier as there is in broadcasting or even in the narrowcasting of cable television; nor is there the shared theatrical experience of a cinema. Of all the new technologies, therefore, video is the closest to traditional publishing.

Video and society

(9) On the other hand, there are some powerful social considerations to be balanced against this. Video is viewed on an ordinary television screen, and frequently in a family setting, where it is watched in the same physical manner, if not always in the same mental attitude, as broadcast television. The authority of a medium which carries the national news may, for some viewers, attach to other material which is seen in the home, and this confusion may be particularly acute for pre-teenage children. There is ample evidence that many parents permit their children to watch late-night television, and that some children are permitted to watch adult video as well.

The exploitation of violence

(10) Moving pictures have recently become available in the home which hitherto have been found only in the carefully supervised surroundings of the cinema, where persons

apparently under the age of 18 can for the most part be excluded at the box office, and where the contents of the film can be checked in advance. The new domestic media could make such audience supervision a thing of the past, and the ability of children to view such material in their own sitting rooms or in those of their friends may create problems both for parents and, in time, for society at large. Not only is film a uniquely powerful medium, as the Williams Committee concluded after two years of close examination; it is a teaching medium as well, and the lessons taught by some of the videograms available in Britain this year have been dangerous enough, even to adults, to invite the attentions of the Director of Public Prosecutions.

(11) The trend towards the exploitation of extreme violence and sadism in screen entertainment has already received sufficient comment in the media, but the trend is not a new one. The Williams Committee singled out such material in justifying a continued certification of films even for adults:

> *"We should make the point that the violence we have seen on film (from films refused a certificate, or cut before the film could be certified) far exceeds in nastiness anything likely to be seen on television. It is not simply the extremity of the violence which concerns us: we found it extremely disturbing that highly explicit depictions of mutilation, savagery, menace and humiliation should be presented for the entertainment of an audience in a way that appeared to emphasise the pleasures of sadism. Indeed, some of the film sequences we saw seemed to have no purpose of justification other than to reinforce or sell the idea that it can be highly pleasurable to inflict injury, pain or humiliation (often in a sexual context) on others. Film, in our view, is a uniquely powerful instrument: the close-up, fast cutting, the sophistication of modern make-up and special effects techniques, the heightening effect of sound effects and music, all combine on the large screen to produce an impact which no other medium can create."*
>
> *(Report of the Committee on Obscenity and Film Censorship, Cmnd 7772, paragraph 12.10)*

Violence and obscenity law

(12) The Obscene Publications Act 1959 was designed to impose an ultimate criminal test even on publications designed to be consumed in private, and for many years it was applied in practice largely through the prosecution of erotic or pornographic material. 1982, however, has been notable for the firm line taken by the courts in declaring that the deprave-and-corrupt test of British obscenity law may apply to extremes of violence and sadism as well. When children are among the likely audience for such entertainment, the problem is even greater, and prosecutors have taken the view that the corruption of the young is a proper area for the application of obscenity law in Britain, since the test is whether the material is likely to deprave and corrupt a significant proportion of those who, in all the circumstances, are likely to encounter it.

The protection of children and young persons

(13) The accessibility of video to the young is a major worry. The playback facility on cassette recorders is simple to operate, and there can be few children over the age of 10 who are incapable of mastering it. Moreover, because a videogram is a physical entity, it may lie on a shelf or in a cupboard for a considerable period of time, to be discovered one day by a growing child whose presence was unforeseen when the videogram was acquired. The legitimate tastes of adults may run to material which, on reflection, they would prefer their

children not to see, but the problem of controlling a child's access to adult video is a continuing one. For that reason, parents have a right to expect the clearest possible warning of material which may be damaging to children, and the education of adults in this new age of electronic information may come to seem just as important as the education of children.

(14) In the last resort, there are laws in Britain to protect the young, whether by insisting on the safety of proper fireguards, or by putting children on a risk register when they are alleged to have been battered by a parent. Our Committee recognised that it might be difficult to persuade people who are buying or hiring videograms that there was this fireguard analogy vis-a-vis entertainment intended to be viewed in the home. Nevertheless, we agreed that the welfare of children demanded that parents assume some responsibility for their children's viewing and that shop-keepers agree to pay some heed to the age of customers to whom they either sell or hire adult entertainment.

Prior classification and restricted access

(15) A system of prior classification has two advantages. First, it provides a warning to both parents and shopkeepers of the minimum age which is recommended for the viewing of a particular film or videogram. And second, if properly and effectively administered, it protects the rights of adults to view legitimate adult entertainment without the need to consider the vulnerabilities of a potential audience of children or young people.

(16) The Hunt Committee recommended that no film should be shown on cable television which has not been previously certificated by the British Board of Film Censors, and that the time bars for adult films which have become traditional in broadcast television and which are imposed by licence on the pilot cable schemes should continue. Only one exception was proposed: that separate subscription channels which could provide parents with an electronic locking device might be permitted to show adult films with no restriction on the time of day or because they are unsuitable for children. Furthermore, "it would be acceptable with this safeguard to allow the showing of any film passed by the British Board of Film Censors for public exhibition with an existing censorship category." They clarify this to mean categories in use in the public cinema, since "we do not think it right to go any further and, for example, allow the showing of the kind of film which has hitherto not been passed for public exhibition and has been confined to cinema clubs, or other video material which does not conform to public-service broadcasting requirements of taste and decency." Consistency with Hunt would suggest that if video is to continue to enjoy greater freedom than cable television, it must be on the grounds that the accessibility of adult material to the young and impressionable is subject to firm and reliable control.

The limits of acceptability

(17) The new Cinematograph (Amendment) Act 1982 was introduced in order to regulate the activities of unlicensed cinema clubs, many of which had been showing films featuring torture, rape and violence against women. During the debates on this measure, Members of Parliament were concerned that this same kind of material, which could now be prohibited in adult cinemas, might be finding its way into the home where it could be seen by children. The harmful influence of aggressive pornography is increasingly acknowledged by research from America, and while it has been argued that one such film may do little damage, the cumulative effect of even a small number of such scenes when

deliberately sought out by the disturbed or vulnerable could prove psychologically harmful, especially when the scene can be played back again and again on home video with little or no reference to context.

Violence on television

(18) The dangerous influence of scenes of violence on television has been commented on by both the Annan Committee and by a Government White Paper, and both the BBC and the IBA have issued guidelines on the portrayal of violence on television. Both authorities recognise that even late-night programmes may be watched by unattended children, who may see such programmes as representing, in the words of the BBC's Note of Guidance, "a desirable adult world which they long to enter." And this BBC Report draws particular attention to the plight of those "neglected children who are most likely to imitate violent action." Furthermore, "very young children . . . may not have learned to distinguish between reality and fantasy." The encouraging of violence is an important problem for society, and where "the distinction between heroes and villains has become blurred, . . . conventional morality may be replaced by a tacit acceptance of brutality as a necessary part of 'winning'." Also, "violence in conjunction with the supernatural can be very frightening, especially to immature people, and special signposting should be designed to give proper warning to nervous viewers." Film classification can serve the same purpose.

(19) The IBA's Working Party stresses the distinction "to be drawn between what might be 'disturbing' (or offensive) and what might be harmful." And in commenting on the 'sanitised' or 'conventional' violence sometimes regarded as relatively harmless, it points out that while the impact "on viewers' emotions may be less distressing, its influence on their social behaviour could be equally undesirable. The suggestible and impressionable may be made less sensitive to the real consequences of violence and by such ignorance encouraged in attitudes and possibly even led to commit imitative brutal acts."

(20) Copycat violence amongst children is a particularly worrying phenomenon and the BBC has taken particular care on early-evening television to avoid setting dangerous examples, like "the use of knives or broken bottles in fights, nooses, trip-wires, karate chops, fire-eating, knife-throwing, tying up with ropes, playing on railway lines, climbing up pylons and telegraph poles, or the locking-up of 'prisoners' in outhouses, empty rooms, or cellars or hiding in old refrigerators or ovens." On grounds of social responsibility, broadcast television has also avoided giving the details of drug use and of manufacture of weapons, "especially when the materials may be close at hand; for example, in the case of nail-bombs and Molotov cocktails." A criminological research conference organised by the Council of Europe "stated that violence in films and television programmes does encourage violence and crime, but *only* among those already 'predisposed towards aggression'." Screen violence is not claimed here to be the sole cause of violence in society, but it may be a contributory factor, and the requirement that films and television should not "be likely to encourage or incite crime or to lead to disorder" is a sound and indeed unanswerable one which the video industry cannot ignore if it wishes to gain the trust of society.

Public offensiveness and private choice

(21) The requirement that neither broadcast television nor the cinema should "be offensive to public feeling" is rather more difficult, since offensiveness is largely subjective and will differ from one individual to another. There is a clear distinction for most people in Britain

between a private offence and a public offence, and the Annan Committee in its Report on the Future of Broadcasting recognised that "most people are fairly robust about private offence – something that they and they alone witness. It is when they witness it in the company of others that their own private response is overlaid by social sensitivity and they begin to voice their disquiet." Questions of propriety are largely a matter of what is appropriate to a particular time and place. Thus club cinemas, with a narrow and self-selected clientele, are permitted greater freedom than the public cinema. Video, potentially the most private medium of all, should be able to be judged by the test of private offence, but only if society has confidence that videograms which have been classified for adults are seen only by adults and are not therefore likely to influence either the public behaviour or the private welfare of children or young people.
(22) In considering all these matters, we saw our task as twofold: to devise a system of classification which would provide the most useful information to parents, to consumers generally, and to the trade; and to propose a system of administration which would reassure the public that the category system could be trusted and that its terms and conditions would secure a reasonable degree of compliance from publishers, distributors and retailers. The crucial first step in social responsibility, we felt, was to introduce some controls at the point of sale.

A System of Classification
Consumer Information
(23) In devising a category system for retail products, we had to consider first the sort of information which might be needed. Should we, for example, attempt to identify the contents of a film in terms of genre, or should we merely indicate the appropriate minimum age? If the latter, how many different age categories could the shopkeeper reasonably be expected to handle, and should these be chosen for video alone, or be the ones familiar from the cinema and from cable TV as well.

On the first point, we agreed that it would be useful if the pack contained some indication of the genre, like a horror film or a Western, but that this need not be included in the category symbol. These certificates, if they are to be readily understood, ought to be as close as possible to those in use at the cinema. BBFC categories have always been based primarily on audience age, although some adults prefer to use them as a warning of the sort of material they themselves might wish to avoid. In the case of video, it seems likely that many customers would appreciate the same sort of early-warning system, particularly when the judgment is provided by an independent body whose opinions they have come to know and trust. The descriptions provided through advertising are not intended for this purpose, since some companies will prefer not to stress the possibly offensive nature of their films, whilst others may choose to emphasise their salaciousness or their gory violence for publicity purposes. Cinema categories, by their very familiarity, have known parameters, and video customers would find them as useful as audiences for cable or satellite television.

Age categories – how many and why?
(24) We considered how many categories were needed, and whether there might be fewer for a retail medium than for the cinema. At least one category, we felt, had to be reserved for adult viewing, but we questioned whether this should be set at 16 or 18. Our view was that the raising of the 'X' certificate age from 16 to 18 in 1970 had been appropriate, given the nature of some of the adult entertainment which had become available. The treatment of

rape and sexual violence in the cinema could, we felt, be disturbing to teenagers, and particularly to girls, who were just discovering their own sexuality. Knowledge, we felt, was important to teenagers, but some forms of experience could be deeply disturbing if encountered too early, and films which exploit or explore in some detail certain aspects of immorality or anti-social violence were better reserved for true adulthood.

(25) If 18, then, was a necessary age category for some videograms, was there a need for another category as few years younger? On the whole, we felt there was, since teenagers were ready to sample the adult world long before they were ready to come to terms with its most painful experiences. We also realised that if there were no mid-teens category, simply a generalised warning about material that could trouble some children, then we risked suggesting that pre-teenagers had the same capacity for experience as adolescents. On the whole, we concluded that gradations of maturity were recognised by most teenagers and by all parents, and we looked for a category system which would give as much information about age suitability as possible. This the current cinema categories had attempted to provide.

(26) On the other hand, when we considered how this information could be most easily assimilated, it seemed to us essential that it be presented in a form which is simple, unambiguous, and memorable. By these criteria, we decided the categories in use since 1970 left much to be desired.

(27) The urgent need at that time had been to raise the age for 'X' films from 16 to 18, but other changes were brought in as well. The old 'A' category was split into 'A' and 'AA', but these two categories had never fixed their meanings clearly in the public mind. Also, the category symbols used in the cinema were all letters of the alphabet, although these were not clearly abbreviations of anything. The 'U', which had once meant Universal (and could now mean Unrestricted) was translated on the category board outside cinemas as: "Passed for General Exhibition." The 'A', which had originally meant Adult and had gradually acquired the licensing condition that children under 16 might attend only if accompanied by a parent or guardian, was now an advisory category informing parents "that the film contains material they might prefer their children under 14 not to see." The 'AA', originally conceived to denote, "adult accompaniment", now simply meant that no children under 14 would be admitted to the cinema, whether accompanied or not. Indeed, no category any longer required adult accompaniment of children, though some parents, and many newspapers, believe it does. The 'X', at least, is recognised as barring those under 18, although the letter 'X' has long been assumed by many non-cinemagoers to denote primarily sex films

(28) The Williams Committee suggested changing this system in the interests of clarity, with numerical ages where possible as used throughout the rest of Europe. Thus 'X' would be changed to (18), a neutral label and instantly comprehensible. For the 'AA' category, Williams suggested raising the minimum age from 14 to 16, since 14, falling right in the middle of puberty for many children, could be an age of maximum sexual confusion, with glandular changes racing ahead of emotional development, and making it difficult for 14-year-olds to see themselves as either children or budding adults. Williams recommended 16, the official school-leaving age and the age of sexual consent, but both the film industry

and the local authorities had felt that this was too close to 18 for easy discrimination at the box office. The BBFC proposed 15 as an acceptable compromise, which would at least be post-puberty for most children, and this we accepted.

Age bars for more than one category

(29) We next consider whether the (15) category should be restrictive, like the (18), or merely advisory. We recognised that once the videogram arrives in the home the label will be only advisory, but we felt that a label which is restrictive in the shops would be taken by most parents as strong advice rather than weak advice. We also felt that some subjects of legitimate interest to teenagers ought not to be made accessible to younger children. Where violence is concerned, we agreed with the broadcasting authorities that it was important not to normalise certain kinds of anti-social behaviour in videos which would be available to early adolescents who were passing through the highly impressionable and difficult phase which occurs at about 13 or 14. We were worried, too, about the extent to which casual drug-taking, and particularly the use of cannabis, had become normal in many American films which could not, in other respects, be classified as suitable only for adults. We did not feel that casual drug use should be normalised or legitimised for that very vulnerable group of young teenagers who were most prone to mindless copycat behaviour.

The shopkeeper's responsibility

(30) We were aware that the imposition of more than one category restricted by age might cause difficulties for untrained shop assistants, but we felt that if box-office staff could learn to enforce these categories in the cinema, then retail staff could do the same. Our researches revealed that British law already prescribed more than one minimum age for products or activities considered potentially dangerous. Driving licences are graded by age: at 14 for electrically assisted pedal bikes, at 16 for mopeds, and at 17 for motorcars and motorcycles. Teenagers may marry at 16, but neither vote nor enter a betting shop until 18. For fireworks and cigarettes, the minimum age is 16, for alcohol 18. Gradations of maturity are recognised by law as well as being understood by most teenagers, and we felt that society would have the right to expect video shopkeepers to assume the same responsibilities as the law now requires retailers to do for these other products.

A new category for adult shops

(31) We examined the range of material currently available on video and agreed that some of it was of a kind which society would not wish to see included in the public categories, even where restricted to persons of 18 and over. Films of a kind shown only in cinema clubs ought not, we felt, to be available in retail outlets which were frequented by the young; and here we agreed with the Williams Committee that such material would be most acceptable if restricted to special shops to which no one under the age of 18 was admitted. The licensing of cinema clubs would involve the introduction of a 'club category' for films, and some comparable arrangement seemed appropriate for videograms which could be exhibited, sold or hired only in segregated premises to which persons under the age of 18 were not admitted. The Williams Report had proposed such a category both for films of quality which were too explicit for general release and for films of no merit which need not be prohibited absolutely and which adults should be able to see if they so choose. Of course, such videograms would still be subject to any limits imposed by law, but access to them would be restricted.

(32) During the course of our deliberations, a new piece of legislation was debated in Parliament which would require the licensing of all 'sex shops', a term defined so as to include shops which specialise in the sale or hire of video or sound recordings dealing primarily with explicit sex or violence related to sex. This Local Government (Miscellaneous Provisions) Act is now law, and the consequence will be that the number and locations of such shops may be limited and that terms and conditions may be imposed on them by the local authority. Parliament has decreed that 'sex articles' should be more difficult to acquire than in recent years and have done so by imposing controls at the point of sale. Thus our proposed category for videograms of this type may now be restricted by law to those dealers specially licensed under the terms of this Act.

Advisory junior categories

(33) Having agreed on three categories which it would be reasonable to treat as limited by age, we felt that the junior and more general categories could be advisory only. Parents are generally the best judge of what their pre-teenage children are ready for, and not all parents worry about the same things. Those who are most concerned about violence in entertainment may feel less troubled about mild instances of bad language or occasional glimpses of nudity in a non-sexual context, both of which are seen as questions of manners rather than morals. The cinema categories 'U' and 'A', we felt, were adequate, provided they could be more clearly explained, and here we were happy to see the film industry adopt a revised system of public categories which did just that.

The new cinema categories – a multi–media approach

(34) The new system of cinema categories, to be introduced in December 1982, embodies virtually all of our proposals, and the list of public categories is as follows:

U – UNIVERSAL. Suitable for all.

PG – PARENTAL GUIDANCE. Some scenes may be unsuitable for young children.

15 – Passed only for persons of 15 years and over.

18 – Passed for persons of 18 years and over.

These categories were designed for multi-media use, and the Hunt Committee proposed their application to cable TV on an official basis.

An additional children's category for video

(35) The one modification which we felt might be useful for video was an indication of some distinction between films suitable for all and those which were particularly suitable for children. The film industry felt that this distinction was not necessary in the cinema, where advertising could give an indication of the target age and where 'U' films were generally aimed at the widest possible audience. With video, however, a shopkeeper might wish to stock a special children's section, as in a bookshop, and our Working Party agreed that, should this labelling be considered useful by the publisher, it would be possible for the pack to carry a small 'c' after the 'U', indicating its particular suitability for the young.

UNIVERSAL. Particularly suitable for children.

A 'club category' for the cinema, and its application to video

(36) The anticipated club category for the cinema is now to be introduced as well, and will be designated: 'Restricted 18'. Licensing conditions will restrict this category to segregated premises to which no one under the age of 18 is admitted, and where such a cinema is permitted in a multi-screen complex, it will have to have a separate entrance and no common foyer, refreshment areas or lavatories shared by children attending other films in that complex. We recommend that videograms in the Restricted 18 category should be sold under similar restrictions, to be designated as follows:

RESTRICTED 18 — For restricted distribution only, through segregated premises to which no one under the age of 18 is admitted.

The category symbols: colour-coding, shape-coding, and copyright

(37) The presentation of the categories, we believe, will be as important as the nomenclature, and we recommend the use of colour-coding and shape-coding reminiscent of shapes and colours significant in other fields. Advisory categories, we suggest, should be presented in a triangle, like warning signs in the Highway Code, with mandatory categories in a circle. Traffic signs might provide the analogy for colours as well, with green for U, amber for PG, and red for Restricted. And if the labels were similarly presented in all media, this would fix them more rapidly in the public mind. We also suggest that cateogory symbols should be protected by copyright.

The reasons for the category: a brief précis

(38) Additional information for the consumer could be provided in a box next to the category label. This should include an indication of the genre, a brief précis of the theme (subject to the approval of the publisher), and a clear indication of the reasons for the category given: for example, strong language, incidents of violence or horror, or sexual themes or visuals. Such information should be simple as well as brief, with a maximum of thirty words, and should be purely descriptive and not critical. Its object should be to provide neutral consumer information, and it should not be permitted to seem a form of advertising.

Rejected material

(39) We considered whether a category should be provided for videograms refused a certificate, but decided against this, since it might simply enhance the marketability of such product for certain dealers. Material judged to be in breach of the law would be rejected outright, and a list of such titles would be provided to members of the trade associations and to any other dealers requesting them.

The process of classification, and the obligations which follow

(40) A videogram should always be classified first in the form in which it is submitted, although where the decision is marginal as between two categories, the publisher should be consulted about the certificate desired and about whether he is prepared to make alterations in the interests of a particular classification. Where cuts are possible in order to ensure legality or to conform with the desired certificate, a modified version must be resubmitted for classification. If passed, this should normally become the only form in which that material can be traded under the category assigned. No videogram which carries a BBFC certificate on the screen, the pack, or in advertising copy may differ from the version passed by the Board in that category, unless the fact that it is an amended version is clearly stated in

the publicity and on the packaging, and this new version has also gone through the certification process.

(41) Some videograms of an educational or instructional nature will so clearly be appropriate for the 'U' category that no pre-vetting should be necessary. For these, a form of declaration will be drafted through which the publisher may describe the contents of the videogram and request a self-administered 'U'. If, subsequently, this declaration is proved to be false in any respect, the certificate will be withdrawn and no further declaration accepted from that publisher.

(42) The classification of home video is a new approach and may seem to some sections of the trade to be unnecessary. Some companies have already included "warnings" in the advertising or on the pack, but these, we felt, can easily be construed as more of a challenge to the customer, and inducement rather than a deterrent. There are some consumers for whom product labelling will be sufficient to warn them off contents they wish to avoid, but it is questionable whether children can ever be expected to make such judgments. It was the view of our Committee that society has a right to restrict the freedom of children for their own protection, and this, we felt, must begin at the point of sale.

A Self-Regulatory System of Administration
Alternative means of regulation
(43) The need to encourage general observance of this system of classification was carefully discussed, and three possible approaches were considered:

(a) Statutory

The cinema industry in Britain is subject to licensing controls by the local authorities, and failure to conform to the terms of a certificate may result in prosecution for breach of the licence, removal of a licence being the ultimate sanction. Strict though they seem, these requirements are intended to be reasonable ones, and it is a *reasonable* degree of compliance which is demanded. No cinema proprietor is liable for a failure to demand proof of age in every case, but the terms of the licence stipulate that no person *apparently* below the age specified shall be admitted to any exhibition at which a film with that certificate is to be shown. Obvious or persistent breaches of this rule may result in disciplinary action from the licensing authority.

Licensing controls for video dealers have been proposed by some commentators during the past year. The Home Office has recognised that some sort of statutory framework might be seen as the best solution, but points out that the necessary legislation would inevitably take time.

When Parliamentary Questions have been asked about the compulsory certification of home video, Ministerial replies have stressed that legal requirements could give rise to "serious difficulties of enforcement." Nevertheless, the government is said to be:

". . . Keeping under review the operation of the law in relation to video cassettes in the light, amongst other matters, of the discussions which are taking place between the British Board of Film Censors and the British Videogram Association about the introduction of a certification scheme governing the sale or rental of video cassettes. Should such a scheme be introduced, we would wish to assess its effect before deciding whether any statutory controls were required."
(Patrick Mayhew QC, MP, Minister of State for the Home Department Hansard, 20th October 1982)

It is clear that any voluntary system of self-regulation would need to be carefully framed if it is to reassure those who would at present prefer some system of legal enforcement.

(b) Terms of trade

We also considered whether or not publishers and distributors might impose standard conditions or trade on retailers, which would include compliance with the terms of any certificate which appears on the pack. The difficulty with such a system is that it could be seen by the Monopolies Commission as introducing restrictive practices which would advance the commercial interests of one group of dealers at the expense of another. It is also the case that terms of trade alone would be unlikely to ensure that children were protected, since goods could be traded on to another dealer by a middle-man, leaving no direct contractual relationship between the publisher and shopkeeper. A standards system, if it is to work, must be freely supported by all branches of the video industry so that none of its contractual terms could be construed as in restraint of trade.

(c) Self-regulation – a Video Code of Practice

Codes of Practice are common in Britain, and the degree of uniformity achieved by this voluntary approach to self-regulation has been much admired by countries with no comparable tradition of self-administered rules. Both the Press Council and the Advertising Standards Authority have been successful in securing high standards of professionalism and public accountability from their respective industries, and the Office of Fair Trading now encourages the widest possible use of Codes of Practice in British business. Thus the video industry would be following in a highly reputable tradition if it did the same.

The Voluntary Character of a Code of Practice

(44) The essence of a Code of Practice is that it is voluntarily subscribed to by an entire industry or profession, and it is essential therefore that the details of such a Code are ratified by all those whose business will be affected by it. In the case of the video industry, a Code would affect the day-to-day operations of publishers, distributors and retailers, and it would be useful if trade associations representing all these sectors were to be consulted during the drafting stage. Of course, it would still be open to individual firms to remain outside the self-regulatory system, in which case such traders would be subject, as now, to control only the criminal law. Some publishers or dealers might consider this preferable, but if the industry wishes to maintain a reasonable degree of responsibility for its own housekeeping, then there would clearly be an advantage in securing the widest possible degree of conformity to a voluntary system of self-regulation.

The purpose of a Code of Practice

(45) The first requirement of a Code of Practice is that it sets out in detail the rules which an industry agrees to follow in order to ensure that individuals or firms in that industry conduct their affairs in accordance with responsible professional and commercial standards. A Code of Practice recognises the legitimate public interest in the good conduct of an industry and indicates the means whereby that industry will demonstrate that its trading practices can be trusted.

The Contents of a Code of Practice for the Video Industry

(46) Any voluntary Code of self-imposed rules must make it clear that the law of the land can in no way be superseded by voluntary agreements. The law must be observed in all its aspects, and it is essential that the video industry recognise this fact in the rules it draws up for itself. The law will apply not only to the contents of a videogram, but to the manner in which it is advertised or traded. In particular, it may apply to the deliberate or negligent trading to children of adult videograms which the courts may find damaging to the physical, mental or moral well-being of the young. For that reason, it is essential that all publicity and packaging make clear the minimum age of the target audience.

(47) The Code should specify the details of the category system agreed by the video industry and specify also the implications of each category for the retailer. Adult videos should not be traded to persons apparently below the age specified in the certificate, nor should scenes from such a videogram be exhibited in any section of a shop to which children have access. Parents may take great exception to adult video being made accessible to children without their permission, and video traders may lose the goodwill of their communities if they fail to take note of such feelings.

(48) It is important that the Code should specify the means by which the rules agreed by the industry can be most widely disseminated, since it is through knowledge of the Code and reference to its terms that the self-regulating trader will normally conduct his affairs. Copies of the Code should be distributed in the first instance through the trade associations subscribing to it, and it is to their own trade associations that traders will normally turn when in doubt about matters of interpretation. It should also be possible for any non-affiliated shop or firm to receive a copy of the Code on request.

(49) Since videograms may be sold in such outlets as supermarkets, greengrocers, or petrol stations, the industry will not be able to anticipate a professional degree of expertise from shop assistants, few of whom will have any previous experience of dealing with screen entertainment. For that reason, the certificate must do the work for them, and its terms must, as far as possible, be self-explanatory, not only to retail staff, but to customers. The category system recently adopted by the film industry was designed with video in mind. Where letters are used, they are abbreviations for words which will appear next to the symbol, and where a number appears in a circle, this refers to the minimum age of customers to whom the videograms may be sold or hired. The list of categories should be displayed in all shops for the convenience of customers and staff.

(50) Where a film has been refused a certificate, dealers should be informed, and the proprietor of any video shop subscribing to the Code should be expected both to understand its terms and conditions and to refuse to stock any videogram if advised of its rejection. Distributors subscribing to the Code should also undertake not to handle such rejected material, although they should be free to modify their product so as to make it acceptable in law for trading under the terms of whatever certificate is found appropriate. Distributors should also undertake not to release a videogram for which they hold a certificate in a form which is different from that to which the certificate was granted.

(51) Neither the category system agreed by the industry nor the Code of Practice through which it is administered should be considered permanent or immutable. Circumstances change, and the precise terms of trade which are found to be practicable may change as well. It should therefore be possible for the video industry to discuss whatever changes are required in their own Code of Practice and to amend the Code as required. The trade associations will be the most appropriate medium through which to discuss any changes which become necessary, and these associations will also provide the appropriate first level for ensuring a reasonable degree of compliance with the Code. What seems less likely, however, is that the trade associations will prove appropriate for the tasks of industry – wide co-ordination and public accountability which will inevitably arise, and it would thus be advisable for the industry to consider some supervisory mechanism for administering the Code.

Functions and possible structure for a Video Standards Council

(52) It is customary in Britain for Codes of Practice to be administered by independent bodies whose primary responsibility is the supervision of standards. Trade associations have as their primary concern the commercial interests of their members, and the public responsibilities of a profession or industry have frequently been allocated to an independent council. Thus the General Medical Council is distinct from the British Medical Association, the Press Council from both the Newspaper Society and the Newspaper Publishers Association, and the Advertising Standards Authority from the Advertising Association and the Institute of Practitioners in Advertising. By analogy, the video industry might like to consider the setting up of an indpendent organisation, which could perhaps be called the Video Standards Council.

(53) The primary function of such a council would be to consider not the commercial interests of video traders in isolation, but their duties to each other, as responsible traders, and to the public whose interest must never be ignored. If the Code of Practice is carefully framed, the Council would be able to concentrate in the first instance on the extent to which the terms of the Code are observed by all firms or individuals subscribing to it. It would do this by monitoring just how far firms in the industry are seen by the public as complying with the Code, and it would investigate complaints from within the industry about breaches of any of its rules. Such a complaint might, for example, be by one retailer against a competitor in the same neighbourhood who had persistently flouted the Code in order to gain an unfair commercial advantage. The Council could also apply whatever sanctions it thought fit to ensure conformity, and could make its decisions public where this was felt to be necessary.

The adjudication of complaints

(54) The adjudication of complaints from both within the industry and without would be an essential function of the Video Standards Council. If it is agreed that industry complaints can properly be dealt with by the industry itself, then the Council could establish an industry sub-committee to investigate such complaints. Members of this sub-committee could be directly appointed by the trade associations so that internal enforcement of the Code remains self-regulatory in all aspects. The Advertising Standards Authority does not employ its independent adjudicators to investigate complaints from within the advertising industry, these being dealt with by the Code of Advertising Practice Committee, which consists exclusively of persons nominated by the professional and trade associations

subscribing. It is this Committee which then applies whatever sanctions may be thought necessary.

Public accountability

(55) In any industry, there will from time to time be conduct which gives rise to complaints from the public, and it is for this reason that bodies like the Press Council and the Advertising Standards Authority are constituted so as to have an independent Chairman appointed from outside the industry, and a majority of Council members who are independent of any interest in that industry. The Advertising Standards Authority requires that the appointment of its Chairman be approved by the Secretary of State for Trade, and the same approach is taken by the British Board of Film Censors, also an unofficial body, whose President and Secretary have their appointments approved not only by the film industry, but by the local authorities and the Home Secretary of the day. Some similar procedure might be advisable for the video industry in selecting a Chairman for the Video Standards Council, and this independent Chairman could then have the right to choose the lay members of the Council, who would constitute a majority. Since Council members would have in turn to ratify the appointment of a new Chairman, the public interest would be seen to be catered for on a continuing basis.

(56) Since the investigation of complaints would be the primary responsibility of the top tier of any Video Standards Council, it would be necessary for the Council to ensure that its decisions are binding throughout the industry. In general, if the Code and the Council are functioning properly, reputable firms and individuals would wish to be seen as complying with the findings of their own self-governing body, and for that reason the publication of judgments by the Council would normally be found to be the only sanction which is required in the majority of cases. Both the Advertising Standards Authority and the Press Council have used the publication of judgments in this manner, and there is no reason to believe that the video industry would not come to see its own interests in the same light. In a few cases, however, there may be recalcitrant traders whom the rest of the industry would wish to discipline for repeated flouting of the industry's own rules. Here again, publicity might prove the most effective sanction.

(57) Each retail shop which subscribes to the Code should display prominently in its window a notice indicating that: "This shop observes the Code of the Video Standards Council," and the ultimate sanction might be the removal of accreditation by the Council, with due publicity given to the fact that the Council believes the shop or firm to be trading in a manner which is unacceptable to the industry as a whole. The isolation of such a trader and the consequent bad publicity might invite the attentions of law-enforcement agencies to the manner in which the business is carried out and to the nature of the videograms which are made available there to the public, and this, too, could have its effect. Any further sanctions would be left to the courts, should these prove necessary or appropriate.

A Publicity and Packaging Committee

(58) The offensiveness of some video advertising in 1982 led the British Videogram Association itself to refer certain cases to the Advertising Standards Authority, and in every one of these complaints, the Authority supported the BVA's view that these advertisements reflected no credit on the industry nor on the companies which had sponsored them. A Code of Practice for the video industry should stipulate that the Video Standards Council maintain a Publicity and Packaging Committee to control standards in this highly contentious field.

(59) The film industry has for many years maintained a Poster Committee which meets weekly in order to pre-vet all publicity for 'X' films (now '18'). Under the new cinema category system it will probably be necessary for this Committee also to approve publicity for films in the (15) category. Industry publicity departments are represented on this Committee, as are distributors and exhibitors, but the media are represented as well through the Newspaper Society and London Transport Advertising. Since the beginning of 1979, the British Board of Film Censors and the Advertising Standards Authority have also been represented, the latter through the Code of Advertising Practice Committee.

(60) Some industries have accepted the pre-vetting of all packaging and advertising on a voluntary basis, as for example the pharmaceutical industry through its trade association, the Proprietary Association of Great Britain. A comparable task should be undertaken by the video industry, although for reasons of practicality it might be agreed that only videograms in the restricted categories need have their copy approved in advance. Material in the 'Restricted 18' category might be subject to further, legal constraints through the Local Government (Miscellaneous Provisions) Act and the Indecent Displays (Control) Act, and it is probable that the British Board of Film Censors will make approval of packaging for this category a condition of certification.

(61) A point to be remembered in assessing the acceptability of either publicity or packaging is its relevance to obscenity law. Already this year, the advertising for videograms subsequently found obscene by the courts has been noted as designed to appeal to the basest instincts of potential customers. Since the test of obscenity is the tendency of a publication to deprave and corrupt a significant proportion of those who are likely to encounter it, it is essential that the expectations of consumers are not influenced in such a way as to make them seek out precisely those sensational elements in a video film which are felt by the courts to be depraving and corrupting. The ease with which scenes of violence or horror may be watched again and again out of context means that their meaning can be structured not by the artistic context but by the expectations created by the advertising or the pack, a consideration which applies far more to video than to the cinema.

(62) All video advertising should conform to the Code of Advertising Practice, administered under the general supervision of the Advertising Standards Authority, the rules of which require that advertisements in Britain should be legal, decent, honest and truthful. An awareness of the meaning of these tests should be a normal responsibility of the Publicity and Packaging Committee, which should be able to insist on the withdrawal of copy which is not approved and the resubmission of revised copy until the Committee is satisfied. Appeals from the decisions of the Publicity and Packaging Committee could be considered by the Video Standards Council, whose judgment would be final.

Free movement of goods in the EEC

(63) A regulatory system which requires that all imported videograms, including those from EEC countries, should be routed through UK distributors may be seen as constituting a non-tariff barrier to imports in violation of Article 30 of the EEC Treaty and equivalent provisions of the EEC agreements with the EFTA countries. A video Code of Practice, therefore, including the rules on packaging, must be applied in such a way as not to constitute a financial or other impediment to such direct import by retailers, film societies, etc.

Freedom of expression

(64) Because of the voluntary nature of a Code of Practice, compliance will always be voluntary, and the Code should never be used to breach the legitimate exercise of freedom of expression as guaranteed by Article 10 (1) of the European Convention on Human Rights. But the video industry should be aware that the Convention goes on to say in article 10 (2) that this freedom "may be subject to such formalities, conditions, restrictions or penalties as are necessary in a democratic society . . . for the prevention of disorder or crime [or] for the protection of health of morals . . ."

Conclusion

(65) In all our deliberations, we have been aware of the need to devise a scheme which would ensure an appropriate balance between the rights and responsibilities of this important new medium of publishing. On the one hand, we believe that the video trade should attempt to provide the maximum informed choice to its customers, while, on the other, it should ensure, as far as possible, that its products are unlikely to be misused or to fall into the wrong hands so as to become a disturbing or anti-social influence on the young, the vulnerable, or the irresponsible.

(66) Many organisations and agencies of government, central and local, have expressed an interest in seeing some system of regulation devised for the video industry. In assessing the alternatives, we quickly realised that no system, not even a statutory one, could be foolproof. There will always be traders so lacking in social responsibility that their activities must be controlled by the criminal law. Taken as a whole, however, the video industry is aware that its growing importance in the world entails a certain effort at putting its own house in order. We hope that the system of classification and regulation proposed by us will enable this new industry to flourish, while also reassuring those who have had misgivings about its future development.

(67) Our recommendations for a Video Code of Practice are attached. Once such a Code has been adopted, every effort should be made by firms subscribing to it to phase out the old uncertificated product as soon as new packs become available, and to stock from then on only such videograms as have been granted a certificate and been labelled accordingly.

Recommendations for a Video Code of Practice

This Code sets out in detail the rules which members of trade associations in the British video industry have agreed to follow in order to fulfill their responsibilities both to their customers and to society.

All retail shops subscribing to the Code will have a copy available on demand for the information of both customers and staff.

The provisions of the Code are intended to apply the law and also to complement it. They are not intended to supersede it, and law must have the last word in every case.

The Code is a voluntary one, freely accepted by members of the video industry. For those who accept its rules, the intentions behind them are as important as the words which express them; the spirit is as important as the letter.

1. No publisher, distributor or retailer should knowingly deal in videograms which are in breach of the law; nor should any videograms encourage or incite to crime.

2. No videogram which is legal in itself should be advertised or traded in such a manner as to disregard or flout the legitimate interests of the consumer or of society at large.

3. Videograms which are appropriate and legal for an adult audience may be unsuitable for children, and all concerned should be aware that videograms which may lead to the physical, mental or moral harm of children may be judged as criminal if they are allowed to fall into the hands of children through the deliberate policy of the publisher or the negligence of the retailer.

4. Video traders operating under this Code will handle only videograms which have been clearly labelled according to the system of certification agreed for the video industry, and this list of categories will be prominently displayed in every shop.

5. All video advertising and packaging will clearly stipulate the category in which the videogram has been passed by the British Board of Film Censors.

6. The four categories which apply in the public cinema and also on cable TV will apply to videograms sold in shops to which all the public have access. These are:

U – UNIVERSAL. Suitable for all.

PG – PARENTAL GUIDANCE. Some scenes may be unsuitable for young children.

15 – Passed only for persons of 15 years and over.

18 – Passed only for persons of 18 years and over.

7. Categories in a triangle are advisory only and indicate videograms which may be sold or hired to customers of any age.

8. Videograms in the U category which are particularly recommended for children may have a small "c" added on the packet at the discretion of the publisher, i.e.:

Uc – UNIVERSAL. Particularly suitable for children.

9. Categories in a circle are limited by age, and no dealer should sell or hire a videogram in the (15) or (18) categories to anyone apparently below the age specified.

10. No scenes from a videogram in one of the limited categories should be played in any section of a shop to which children have access at that time.

11. A further, more restricted category will be possible for videograms available only from adult shops to which no one under the age of 18 is admitted. If such shops are in the same building as a shop which is open to the public, they must have a separate entrance and a notice stating that no persons below the age of 18 may enter. Videograms in all categories may be traded in such premises, but there will be an additional right to handle material in the category used in the cinema for films to be shown only in licensed clubs or the exhibition areas of licensed sex shops. This category is designated as follows:

RESTRICTED 18 — for restricted distribution only, through segregated premises to which no one under the age of 18 is admitted.

Shops which specialise in this category will require a licence under the Local Government (Miscellaneous Provisions) Act 1982.

12. No videogram in any of the three age-bar categories may be dispensed from an automatic vending machine which is accessible to children.

13. All packaging for videograms not classified 'U' will include a brief indication of the nature of the contents and the reason for the certificate given.

14. No videogram which has been refused a certificate will be handled by dealers who have subscribed to the Code.

15. Where a videogram is found to have been released by the holder of the certificate in a form different from that to which the certificate was granted, that certificate may be withdrawn forthwith.

16. Administrative responsibility for applying the Code is vested in the Video Standards Council, which is constituted by agreement with the trade associations and professional bodies subscribing to it. These associations will co-ordinate their activities and those of their members in order to achieve uniformity of standards within the industry, and will assist the Council in up-dating the Code in the light of changing circumstances.

17. Copies of the Code will be widely distributed, and all firms accepting accreditation from the Council will undertake to abide by the Code and to secure the guidance of their trade associations in cases of doubt.

18. All shops subscribing to the Code will display an approved notice prominently in the window to indicate that: "This shop observes the Code of the Video Standards Council."

19. The Council will have an independent Chairman appointed by the member associations with the approval of the Secretary of State for Trade. The Chairman will supervise the appointment of other members of the Council, a majority of whom will be independent of any interest in the video industry, and the appointment of a new Chairman will be ratified by current members of the Council.

20. The Video Standards Council will monitor the extent to which the terms of the Code are observed by all firms or individuals subscribing to it.

21. Members of the Council will adjudicate on all complaints arising from the conduct of any firm or individual in the video industry. Complaints from the public will be dealt with by a panel the majority of whom will be independent of any interest in the video industry. The judgments of the Council in such cases will be made public in whatever form the Council think appropriate. Complaints from within the video industry may be dealt with by a panel all or most of whom are nominated by the trade associations from within the video industry. Adjudications on such complaints may be made public at the discretion of the Council.

22. A Publicity and Packaging Committee will meet weekly as required to vet copy and pictorial material intended for use in connection with videograms in the (15) and (18) categories. Media representatives will be included on this Committee, as will independents, including representatives of the British Board of Film Censors and the Code of Advertising Practice Committee, which operates under the aegis of the Advertising Standards Authority.

23. Copy which has been found unacceptable by the Publicity and Packaging Committee will be withdrawn, and revised copy will be submitted until approval has been obtained.

24. Appeals from the decisions of this Committee will be considered by the Video Standards Council.

25. The Council may take such steps as are necessary to ensure compliance with the Code, including the enforcement of penalties against individuals or firms who fail to comply with its rules.

26. Persistent breaches of the Code may result in the removal of accreditation by the Council, with due publicity given to the fact that the Council believes the shop or firm in question to have been trading in a manner which is unacceptable to the industry as a whole.

27. No provision of this Code should be used to abridge the legitimate exercise of freedom of expression as guaranteed by Article 10 (1) of the European Convention on Human Rights. But the video industry should be aware that the Convention goes on to say in Article 10 (2) that this freedom "may be subject to such formalities, conditions, restrictions or penalties as are necessary in a democratic society . . . for the prevention of disorder or crime [or] for the protection of health or morals . . ."

Report of the Working Party on Videogram Classification

The British Videogram Association has revised the recommended Code of Practice which was drawn up by the Working Party and which appears on pages 23 – 25 of the Report. The revised Code appears on the following pages (nos 27–30) and it is this latter Code which the BVA will recommend the Videogram Standards Council to adopt.

The B.V.A. Videogram Classification Code
As of April 1983

This Code sets out in detail the rules which members of trade associations in the British videogram industry have agreed to follow in order to fulfil their responsibilities both to their customers and to society.

All retail shops subscribing to the Code will have a copy available on demand for the information of both customers and staff.

The provisions of the Code are intended to apply the law and also to complement it. They are not intended to supercede it, and the law will have the last word in every case.

The Code is a voluntary one, freely accepted by members of the videogram industry. For those who accept its rules, the intentions behind them are as important as the words which express them; the spirit is as important as the letter.

1. No publisher, distributor or retailer should knowingly deal in videograms which are in breach of the law.

2. Videograms which are appropriate and legal for an adult audience may be unsuitable for children, and all concerned should be aware that videograms which may lead to the physical, mental or moral harm of children may be judged as criminal if they are sold or rented to children through the deliberate policy of the publisher of the negligence of the retailer.

3. All the videogram packaging will show the category in which the videogram has been passed by the appropriate authority. It is proposed that the category symbols should appear on both the cassette and its display box. On the latter the circular symbols should be at least 1.5 cm in diameter and the triangular symbols should have sides of at least that length. The symbols need not appear in colour but where colours are used they are to be those used in the Report of the Working Party.

4. From the date of its commencement, video traders operating under this Code will handle only those newly released videograms which have been clearly labelled according to the system of certification agreed for the videogram industry, and this list of categories will be prominently displayed in every shop. All previously released material will fall into line as quickly as possible, and no later than a date to be decided by the Videogram Standards Council.

5. The four categories which apply to videograms sold in shops to which all the public have access are:

– UNIVERSAL. Suitable for all.

– PARENTAL GUIDANCE. Some scenes may be unsuitable for young children.

– Passed only for persons of 15 years and over.

– Passed only for persons of 18 years and over.

6. Categories in a triangle are advisory only and indicate videograms which may be sold or hired to customers of any age.

7. Videograms in the U category which are particularly recommended for children may have a small "c" added on the packet at the discretion of the publisher, i.e.:

– UNIVERSAL. Particularly suitable for children.

8. Categories in a circle are limited by age, and no dealer should sell or hire a videogram in the (15) or (18) categories to anyone apparently below the age specified.

9. No scenes from a videogram in one of the limited categories should be played in any section of a shop to which children have access at the time, except in a trailer which has been classified "U" or "PG".

10. A further, more restricted category will be possible for videograms available only from adult shops to which no one under the age of 18 is admitted. If such shops are in the same building as a shop which is open to the public, they must have a separate entrance and a notice stating that no persons below the age of 18 may enter.

Videograms in all categories may be traded in such premises, but there will be an additional right to handle material in the category used in the cinema for films to be shown only in licensed clubs or the exhibition areas of licensed sex shops. This category is designated as follows:

RESTRICTED 18 — For restricted distribution only, through segregated premises to which no one under the age of 18 is admitted.

Shops which specialise in this category will require a licence under the Local Government (Miscellaneous Provisions) Act 1982.

11. No videogram in any of the three age-bar categories may be dispensed from an automatic vending machine which is accessible to children.

12. All packaging for videograms not classified "U" may include a brief indication of the nature of the contents and the reason for the certificate given.

13. No videogram which has been refused a certificate will be handled by dealers who have subscribed to the Code.

14. Where a videogram is found to have been released by the holder of the certificate in a form which merits a more restrictive classification than that for which the certificate was granted, that videogram must be withdrawn forthwith.

15. Administrative responsibility for applying the Code is vested in the Videogram Standards Council, which is constituted by agreement with the trade associations and professional bodies subscribing to it. These associations will co-operate their activities and those of their members in order to achieve uniformity of standards within the industry, and will assist the Council in up-dating the Code in the light of changing circumstances.

16. Copies of the Code will be widely distributed, and all firms accepting accreditation from the Council will undertake to abide by the Code and to secure the guidance of the Videogram Standards Council in cases of doubt.

17. All subscribers to the Code will prominently display an approved notice to indicate that: "We observe the Code of the Videogram Standards Council."

18. The Council will have an independent Chairman appointed by the member associations with the approval of the Secretary of State.

19. The Videogram Standards Council will monitor the extent to which the terms of the Code are observed by all firms or individuals subscribing to it.

20. Members of the Council will adjudicate on all complaints relating to videogram classification. Such adjudications may be made public at the discretion of the Council.

21. The Council may take such steps as are necessary to ensure compliance with the Code, including the enforcement of penalties.

22. Persistent breaches of the Code may result in the removal of accreditation by the Council, with due publicity given to the fact that the Council believes the firm or individual in question to have been trading in a manner which is unacceptable to the industry as a whole.

23. No provision of this Code should be used to abridge the legitimate exercise of freedom of expression as guaranteed by Article 10 (1) of the European Convention on Human Rights. But the videogram industry should be aware that the Convention goes on to say in Article 10 (2) that this freedom "may be subject to such formalities, conditions, restrictions or penalties as are necessary in a democratic society . . . for the prevention of disorder or crime (or) for the protection of health or morals . . ."

Index